The Hidden Life

Thoughts on Communion with God

By Adolph Saphir

PANTIANOS
CLASSICS

Published by Pantianos Classics

ISBN-13: 978-1-78987-504-1

First published in 1877

Contents

Preface

The following pages, with the exception of chapters v., vi., and xi., contain the substance of addresses, given in the ordinary course of congregational ministration, on James iv. 8, "Draw nigh to God, and He will draw nigh to you." I have endeavoured to offer a few elementary thoughts on the great subject of the Christian's hidden life, and to describe the experienced reality of revelation and of prayer, or of communion with God.

Much is said and written in the present day in defence of truth against the attacks of unbelief and doubt; much also in the way of appeal and invitation to those who are still strangers to the enjoyment of Christ's peace. While fully admitting the necessity and importance of both these aspects, the apologetic and the evangelistic, we may yet regard as of still greater importance the unfolding of Scripture itself, the testimony of the reality of the things which are freely given to us of God in Christ, and by the Spirit. It is right to guard the house against the attacks of foes, or rather to point out the strength and security of the divinely-laid foundation. It is also right to point out the gate wide and open, and to declare to all the freeness and fulness of divine grace. But to describe the home itself, the inner sanctuary, seems to be more essential, and also more in accordance with the practice of the apostles, who declared the whole counsel of God, and regarded the preaching of the gospel, in its fulness, and with the power of the Holy Ghost, as at once the great argument to convince, and the great attraction to persuade. I have endeavoured to point out in chapters v. and vi. what I regard as the Scripture method of defence of revelation and prayer.

When we meditate on the hidden life, we realize the substantial unity of all who believe in the grace of our Lord Jesus Christ, the love of God, and the communion of the Holy Ghost. We are often astonished that Christians hold doctrinal views which appear to us to be inconsistent with some vital truth, or that they are able to live in communions or churches with which we could not feel at liberty to be connected. But however perplexing this may be, we know that none can call Jesus Lord but by the Holy Ghost; and when we are brought most fully and deeply into communion with Christ, in seasons of great soul-trial or spiritual elevation, we feel most clearly and strongly that there is one spirit which unites all who love the Lord Jesus, and who have experienced the power and sweetness of divine grace. Our want of union and brotherly love arises, it seems to me, not from attaching too much importance to the points in which we differ, but from our not beholding clearly enough, and our not realizing sufficiently the magnitude of the fundamental truth, held by all Christians, *God manifest in the flesh*.

Hoping that these simple pages may, by God's blessing, prove helpful to some believers and seekers, I conclude with the words of an old author, applicable to hearer as well as teacher: "It is a cold, lifeless thing to speak of spiritual things upon mere report; but they that speak of them as their own, as having share or interest in them, and some experience of their sweetness, their discourse is enlivened with firm belief and ardent affection; they cannot mention them (or hear of them) but their hearts are straight taken with such gladness as they are forced to vent in praises." [1]

A. S.

Trinity Presbyterian Church,
Notting Hill,
February, 1877.

[1] Archbishop Leighton.

Chapter One - The Open Secret

"Draw nigh to God, and He will draw nigh to you" - James iv. 8.

NOT every mystic Is a Christian, but every Christian is a mystic.

There Is a *hidden wisdom*. The apostle Paul writes: "We speak wisdom among them that are perfect: yet not the wisdom of this world, nor of the princes of this world, that come to nought: but we speak the wisdom of God in a mystery, even the hidden wisdom, which God ordained before the world unto our glory." [1] The secret of the Lord is with them that fear Him. In the hidden centre of their being God makes them to know wisdom. [2] They have an unction from above, which teacheth them of all things, and is truth. [3] "Knowest thou where wisdom is found? and where is the place of understanding? ...The depth saith, It is not in me: and the sea saith, It is not with me." [4] But Jesus declares that the Father hath revealed it unto babes. [5]

There is a *hidden glory*. It Is manifested, [6] and yet only faith can behold it. Jesus changed the water into wine at the marriage of Cana, and showed forth His glory. Men saw, and yet did not see; but His disciples believed in Him. [7] Jesus raised Lazarus from the grave. There were many witnesses; yet only they who believed saw the glory of God, and the Son of God glorified. [8] The glory of God is beheld by faith in the face of Jesus Christ; [9] and Jesus Christ is known only by those who know the mystery of His cross and resurrection, [10] and are waiting; to be glorified together with Him. [11]

There is a *hidden life,* far, far away — high, high above. It is life hid with Christ in God — life born out of death; as it is written, "For ye have died, and your life is hid." [12] It is mysterious in its commencement. "The wind bloweth where it listeth, and thou hearest the sound thereof, but canst not tell whence it cometh, and whither it goeth: so is every one that is born of the Spirit." [13] It is mysterious in its progress: "I live; yet not I, but Christ liveth in me." [14] It is mysterious in its consummation — the marriage of the Lamb. [15] We shall be for ever with the Lord.

There is a *hidden manna*. We have meat to eat that the world knows not of. [16] "There is an unseen river, the streams whereof make glad the city of God." [17] Only God's children see it, and know the Source whence it cometh, and the Ocean whither It is flowing.

It is impossible to deny the mystical character of Christianity when we consider such passages as these: "If a man love Me, he will keep my words: and my Father will love him, and we will come unto him, and make our abode with him." "Christ will manifest Himself unto us, and not unto the world." "They are not of the world, even as I am not of the world," "The natural man receiveth not the things of the Spirit of God." "Christ dwelleth in the heart by faith." "I labour, striving according to His working, which worketh in me mightily." [18]

If we know these hidden things, then are we ourselves hidden ones, who shall be made manifest when Christ, who is our Life, shall appear. Of this hidden life these pages treat. The soul draws nigh to God; God draws nigh to the soul: the result is communion with God. This is the simplest, the most elementary aspect of the hidden life; and it addresses itself to all. For although wisdom is justified only of her children, although they only hear and understand her voice, yet wisdom speaks to all the words of light and love: "He that hath ears, let him hear." Different from the exclusiveness of human wisdom is the Divine Teacher: He welcomes the simple and the sinful, babes and little children, and all who are bowed down with sorrow, and oppressed with darkness and the shadow of death.

"Drawing nigh to God" is the most comprehensive expression to describe the soul's attitude toward God. Prayer is the culminating point of this attitude. If we rightly view prayer, it embraces our whole life, our thought and feeling, our will and work, our conflict and rest. "Drawing nigh to God" describes the character of the Christian's life. In the meditation of our hearts, in the desires of our soul, in the activities and enjoyments of our daily path, we approach God; for we wish to live before Him, conscious of His presence, in constant dependence and in constant enjoyment of His grace. And "God drawing nigh to us" is the most comprehensive expression to describe God's dealings with us. The Word, or the Scripture, is the great, and in many respects the unique, channel of God's communications to the soul; or rather it is central, round which all other divine influences gather. Scripture is the divine revelation in a special sense, but so that it connects itself with all other manifestations of God to the soul, be they in Nature or Providence, or by the direct influence of the Spirit.

Hence the advice, which is a household word among Christians, that prayer and the reading of Scripture are the great means of sustaining and nourishing the inner life, is perfectly correct, if it is understood in a spiritual and not a mechanical manner, if prayer and Scripture are viewed, not as isolated powers, but as central and culminating points.

There is no safety in distance from God. If we take the wings of the morning and dwell in the uttermost parts of the sea, we cannot go from God's Spirit, nor flee from His presence. Fear of a guilty conscience seeks a hiding-place; but where can we escape the eye of Omniscience, or shield ourselves against the anger of our holy God?

There is only one hiding-place, even God Himself. The only safe place for helpless and sinful men is close to God — in the arms of the Father, at the feet of Jesus, the Friend of sinners, once crucified and now exalted, to give repentance and the remission of sins. Come to Jesus, and thou art in the secret place of the Most High, where no evil can befall thee, nor any plague come nigh thy dwelling. There is no condemnation to them which are in Christ Jesus. The Lord has forgiven all our transgressions, and will remember our sins no more. There is no life, or light, or love in distance from God. Even if man had not fallen, his only happiness and strength would have been in constant dependence on God and communion with Him. In Paradise sinless Adam lived by faith in God. It was in God's light that he saw light, and in receiving constantly the bright and blessed influence of divine love, his spirit rejoiced and was strong in God. No creature is good in itself; no creature has within itself a fountain of life and of blessedness; no creature has even committed to its care a treasure of strength and goodness; but with God is the fountain of life. Constantly beholding the countenance of the Father in heaven, angels and saints are upheld by divine love, and replenished out of the divine fulness.

Now that sin has entered, no effort on man's part can ever bring him nigh to God. Sin has so clouded and darkened the mind, that man cannot rise to the spiritual idea of God; he is always changing the glory of God into the similitude and shadowy image of the creaturely. Jesus is the Image of the invisible God, and in Him all previous revelations of the Name find their ultimate and perfect fulfilment. No human effort could have removed sin as the obstacle between God and us. In Jesus is both deliverance from guilt and the source of renewal. God was in Christ. In the Incarnation, death, resurrection, and the sending forth of the Holy Ghost from the Father, through the glorified humanity of His Son, there is the most perfect fulfilment of the great problem, How can fallen man be brought nigh to God? how can God dwell among and within men? Jesus is the way — the way of God to man, the way of man to God. In Jesus man finds God the Father; in Jesus God finds the lost sheep. Man finds in Jesus God, to have God as his portion; God finds in Jesus man, to be His portion for evermore.

Blessed be God, He has brought us nigh to Himself. We adore the great mystery of godliness, God manifest in the flesh. We rejoice with the joy of broken and healed, of contrite and comforted hearts, because Jesus loved us, and washed us from our sins in His own blood, and brought us near to God, into the Holy of Holies — a royal priesthood. We give thanks for the gift of the Holy Ghost, in whom we now worship the Father, and by whom the light and life has been kindled within our hearts. Herein is love, that, notwithstanding our sin, God has brought us nigh unto Himself. More wonderful and glorious than angelic purity or the innocence of Paradise is the divine righteousness in which we now stand before God; and high above all hopes and thoughts of the human heart are our union with the Incarnate Son of God, and the indwelling of the Holy Ghost in our souls.

"Draw nigh to God, and He will draw nigh to you." The word sounds like a precept, and yet is all promise. At first sight the words have a somewhat legal air, and they who do not understand the deep gospel -spirituality of this epistle might for a moment imagine that this exhortation does not proceed out of the full and living consciousness of grace, and that it implies the thought that man by his own will and exertion can draw nigh to God, who is high above, and by reason of our sin far away. If James required this of us, he would ask not merely what is unevangelical, but impossible. Only attempt to effect nearness to God by your own exertions, when He has departed from you. Give yourselves all possible trouble, you cannot attain and compel it. We enjoy His presence, then, only when He comes of His own accord; this most precious of all gifts none can take to himself."

If it be asked which comes first, our approach to God, or God's approach to us, the answer is evident. Does not this very call of God, Draw nigh, prove that God in His spontaneous and boundless love begins, that in His condescending grace He takes the initiative, that He draws us first by His voice and by His Spirit? Have we chosen Him, or has He chosen us? Has He not loved us with an everlasting love, and is not this the blessed source of His drawing us with loving-kindness? All things are of God. He who was in Christ reconciling the world unto Himself has created us anew in Christ Jesus; He who has made Christ to be wisdom, righteousness, sanctification, and redemption, has also grafted us into the living Vine. "It is not of him that willeth, nor of him that runneth, but of God that showeth mercy." [20]

It is therefore right to say that we must *wait* on God; but waiting on God is not in apathy and indifference; it implies intense activity.

God draws the heart, and the result is the desire of the heart to draw nigh to God. God works in us, but His work in us is to *will*. He delivers us from bondage and apathy; He reveals Himself to us as the living, loving God; He breaks the fetters of dead fatalism; so that instead of dreaming of an abstract and frigid necessity, we behold the God and Father of our Lord Jesus Christ, and hear His voice, "Return unto Me!" We are no longer in the Arctic regions of fatalism; but the Sun of Righteousness shines on us, and we are free. The heart responds to the living God. We *will*, and our face is set toward heaven. Drawing nigh to God is the most concentrated energy of the soul; we are no longer passive, quiescent, but, quickened by the Spirit, we are all desire, longing, and eager expectation; we wait more than they that wait for the morning; we are conscious of our utter dependence on mercy, of our helplessness, of our sin and misery; the heart is broken and contrite, and yet filled with a new and sweet hope; for we feel that though with man it is impossible, with God all things are possible." [21]

When we speak of this influence of divine grace, of the new birth, our testimony, although abundantly proved and illustrated in Scripture, and although it flows from our own experience, meets not only with objections from opponents, but some who are sincerely seeking truth see in this doctrine great and discouraging difficulties. Our object is not to preach 'regeneration,' but to preach Christ; and no difficulty of doctrine, or apparent contradiction of doctrines, can ever come between the voice of God, the call of Jesus, and the sinner needing salvation. The response of the heart is to be given, not to the gospel, but to God, who sends the testimony that Jesus is the Christ, and that eternal life is in Him. Not until the heart is thus brought into contact with Him who says, "Draw nigh to Me," is the gospel-message truly heard.

In a country where Christian truth is constantly explained, there are many who possess an intellectual knowledge of doctrine, who yet have not obeyed the call of God. Their half-knowledge of truth, which can only be fully and correctly understood by believers, often makes it difficult for them to understand the simplicity of the gospel. And in their position much humility and self-distrust will be needed to keep them from cavilling and opposing difficulties. The woman of Samaria, the Ethiopian eunuch, the gaoler of Philippi, and countless multitudes have turned to God in Christ, simply on hearing God's message concerning His Son. They were born again, not by understanding the doctrine of regeneration, but by hearing the voice of God.

When our Lord spoke to Nicodemus, He first showed him how great a matter salvation was. how difficult and above the reach of man, in order then to declare unto him how easy salvation was, how God in His love and by the sacrifice of His Son gave eternal life to whosoever believeth in Jesus. The Spirit of God, of whom Jesus spoke in the first part of His discourse, is not mentioned in the second. And why? Because when man is convinced of his sin, guilt, and helplessness, the Spirit of God enables him to hear the voice of God: "Behold Jesus! Draw nigh to Me!" The sinner, who has given up looking *into himself* for anything good or strong, out of which the new life is to develop, looks now away from himself unto God.

Say not the message, "Ye must be born again," leaves us to hopeless inactivity. It is the message of Him who says, "Look unto Me, and be ye saved, all the ends of the earth." It is addressed to those who, seeking to save and to renew themselves, can find no peace, no help, and it points them to God, to the Spirit, the giver of life. And, going still lower, it is addressed to those who do not as yet know that what they need is grace, not merely to pardon, but to renew. Where sin is truly felt, the necessity of *life* from above is also realized. It is the shallow view of sin which fancies the possibility of self-renewal.

But If you ask the Christian, who by God's grace has drawn nigh, to describe his experience, if you expect a logical and even chronological account of this supernatural and central change, his answer will be: I am most distinctly conscious of the fact of the new birth, I can distinguish between the highest and purest emotions, the most unselfish and generous acts of my natural state and of my old nature, and the new life by faith in Christ. I know that what is born of the flesh is flesh, and what is born of the Spirit is spirit. Christ dwells in my heart by faith; the Spirit of God is in me. To be spiritually-minded is life and peace. Even the word of God, which I knew and admired, reverenced and loved, was formerly outside me, but now it dwells within me. But if you ask *how* and *when* I was born again, I answer, Jesus Himself says that man cannot tell. "The wind bloweth where it listeth, and thou hearest the sound thereof, but canst not tell whence it Cometh, and whither it goeth."

Is not the beginning of all life concealed in sacred and mysterious darkness? And can we expect to analyse this most wonderful of all creations? And when this change is compared to a birth, does not this very comparison point to a still more hidden commencement of life, known only to the Spirit of God? I may remember the culminating point of decision, the efflorescence of the bud, when the heart says, I will draw nigh! or the first conscious reception of vivifying truth; but I am not anxious even about this, nor does it belong to the 'reason' which I am exhorted to be able to give to all who ask me. The Lord draws nigh to the heart, and creates it anew. It is a miracle of grace, and, like all miracles, we see not the process *itself*, but its effect. Once we were dead, now we live; once we were blind, now we see. Jesus, the crucified Saviour, according to His promise, has drawn us unto Himself.

And in this divine change we were set free. Here is no compulsion, but the very reverse of it, emancipation; no limiting or altering of our individuality, but in the strictest sense of the word the commencement of a life personal (or as Scripture expresses it. He called us by *name*), restoration into the original divine idea of our being. If it appears to men otherwise, it is because they forget that it belongs to the very idea and nature of man to be in communion with God, in constant dependence on Him, in the conscious and rejoicing receiving out of His fulness. When God works both to will and to do, then begins our true human existence, our real God-intended individuality, our sweet and dearly-bought freedom. [22]

The most comforting doctrines of grace, and specially of the work of the Spirit, are often changed into difficulties, obstructing the soul's drawing nigh to God, and into excuses [23] for continuing passive. This arises from disobedience to God, who calls; from averting the eyes, which ought to be directed to God in Christ, and which busies itself in introspection, nay, the attempt of eye-inspection. Men turn to the philosophy of looking, to the analysis of the required act of turning unto God. They do not realize that they are called by the living voice; that they have not to deal with doctrines, but with God. But what is the experience of those who yielded to God, although at the very time they were conscious of their sinfulness and their utter dependence on the Spirit of God? It may be compared with the experience of the apostle Peter in prison. Four quaternions of soldiers were keeping him. He was sleeping between two soldiers, bound with two chains. Before the door were keepers guarding the prison. Even if he could have escaped out of these chains and from these keepers, there was the first ward and then the second ward, and beyond that the iron gate that led into the city. Was ever man bound, fettered, and hemmed in so helplessly? But what happened? He arose when the angel commanded him. Noiselessly, easily, the chains fell off from his hands. He passed from the soldiers and the watchmen; he passed through the first and the second ward. The heavy iron gate opened of its own accord. It appeared like a vision, so smooth, silent, and perfect was the deliverance. It is in like manner that the sinner, as soon as he says in his heart, 'Yes' to the heavenly call, as soon as he lifts up his eyes unto the God and Father of our Lord Jesus Christ, finds that all fetters are burst, all keepers are powerless, all barriers are removed. He *does* arise and go to His Father. He *can* pray and weep, thank and rejoice, trust and hope. He draws nigh to God.

"Nothing is more clearly written in Scripture than, on the one hand, that the first upward movements of the soul towards God spring from a prevenient operation of the Spirit of God upon that soul — in other words, that the first pulsations of the spiritual life are divinely set in motion; but, on the other hand, that in the production of this change the soul is absolutely unconscious of any motions save its own. It is because it is 'God which worketh in us both to will and to do' that we are called to 'work out our own salvation.' The instinct of every renewed soul realizes this fact, and his every prayer expresses, in one and the same breath, both the *divine source* and the absolutely *voluntary character* of all his Christian emotions and activities. How the two interact and blend into one is a beautiful subject for thought, but not to be fully apprehended here, and possibly never." [24]

The believer also still needs the constant exhortation and encouragement — "Draw nigh to God, and He will draw nigh to you." The spiritual blessings, which are given to him according to the everlasting covenant, are all treasured up in heavenly places in Christ Jesus. Once we have begun to draw nigh to God, we must always continue to draw nigh. It is both a necessity and our delight. A necessity, because we are still as dependent on the creative, supernatural influence of grace. When David prays, *"Create in me a clean heart,"* this is not the supplication of one who for the first time draws nigh. He teaches us by this expression, "that whether in our regeneration or in our restoration when we have fallen, whatever good is in us is the gift of His grace." [25] We need daily renewing; and whence can this renewing come but from above? It is our delight to draw nigh; for our soul thirsteth after God, the living God. To behold and to enjoy the blessings which are freely given to us in Christ, the believer must continually draw near to God. The beautiful robe of righteousness, the abundant and perfect forgiveness of sin, the glorious adoption of sons, the renewing and upholding influence of the Holy Ghost, the lively hope of the inheritance, behold, they are ours! But let us never think that thought, that memory, that imagination, can bring us into actual possession or enjoyment of them. We must draw nigh to *God,* and He will again bless us with all spiritual blessings.

Again, you must draw nigh to God, that the fruit of the Spirit may be found in you. Has God created you anew in Christ Jesus? has He taken from you the stony heart of unbelief and ingratitude? has He kindled within you love, that love which embraces the Father and the children? has He given you meekness, lowliness, patience? has He caused you to begin the warfare with sin, and the obedience of life? then remember that it is *God* who works all this in you by His Spirit; that it is grace which is disciplining you; that it is not Nature, but the divine life implanted in you, from which all these fruits spring.

And you need to draw nigh unto *God* daily and continually, to abide in Christ, and to have His word abiding in you, that you may continue to glorify God. Such pensioners are we of the Divine bounty, daily and hourly we must be recipients of His gifts and of His power. Peter imagines he has a stock of courage and loving loyalty in himself; but sad experience teaches him that his nature is feeble and selfish; that not he, but Christ in him, is rock. Moses, meekest of all men, cannot of himself conquer the hardness of Israel's unbelief by rising to the all-forgiving gentleness of God. Solomon's wisdom becomes folly; Laodicea imagines herself to have been enriched once for all, and forgets to draw nigh unto *God*. Let those who have received most, continue asking; for we have nothing in ourselves; our sufficiency is of God.

He who has been enriched with spiritual gifts must be brought constantly to feel poor in spirit; for there is the danger of his cleaving to his gifts, and contemplating his gifted self, instead of growing up into Christ, of becoming more rooted in Him who is our only life and strength. We *are* nothing unless we abide in God; we can *do* nothing apart from Christ. We know and admit this as a doctrine; but to realize it as a fact, painful and humbling experience is often needed. But in this lowest humiliation is our true and highest exaltation. God takes all things from us that we may turn again to Him as our sure Portion; He makes us feel our weakness, our poverty, our ignorance, in order that we may return to Him who does not give strength, gifts, and wisdom, but who *is* our light and our salvation. And would we have it otherwise? Do we not love to have it so? Is not God, the giver, more than all His gifts? Is it not an infinitely higher state, that it is not I, but Christ that liveth in me? that it is not I, but the grace of God that worketh in me? that it is not I, but the Spirit, who energises in me effectually?

Is it not beautiful that while God gives us grace to grow and to become strong in Christ, to attain to spiritual manhood, able to discern both good and evil, strong to endure hardness in the warfare, wise to win souls and to labour for the Master, He yet allows us to abide in all the sweet weakness of infancy, resting always calmly on His bosom, and calling forth His motherly tenderness; in the confiding and peaceful humility of childhood, asking for wisdom and guidance, for help and support? The Christian retains what is lovely and beautiful in every age: the mysterious helplessness and sweetness of infancy, the humility and meekness of childhood, the enthusiasm and hopefulness of youth, the matured and sustained strength of manhood, the calmness and wisdom of old age.

"Draw nigh to God," I say thirdly, because, alas! we are often betrayed into sin and forgetfulness of God. We still go astray; we often become weary, and do not resist with all our power. There are seasons of estrangement and of lukewarmness. Sometimes the loving Saviour has to withdraw Himself, and allow us to feel how dreary and bitter it is to forsake Him. Sometimes the soul that has left its first love awakes and finds all dark and cold, and Jesus is absent. Sometimes believers are in danger of becoming proud, hard, self-sufficient, and it is necessary for God to chasten them with leanness in their soul. I feel sure that in all this God is always loving. I feel sure that God would always have us live in the sunshine and joy of His countenance.

Why are these seasons of languor and darkness? The various experiences of the soul are to be traced either to our sins, or to our tendency to claim divine gifts as a right, and to forget that we are always dependent on grace. Their object is to chasten and to restore— -nay, to prepare us for a higher and deeper experience. Only trust Him; for blind unbelief is sure to err. "Draw nigh to God, and He will draw nigh to you."

The journey through the wilderness, which took forty years, might easily have been accomplished in a few days. Ten times Israel tempted the Lord; for years they lapsed into idolatry. We read of Remphan and Moloch in the annals of the chosen people. There is many a night of darkness, many a pang and conflict, into which we bring" ourselves by our own sin, by our yielding to idolatry and conforming with the world. In the Song of Songs we may read a description of the soul's varying experience. That Song does not describe the marriage of the Lamb. The Bride is sometimes in Jerusalem, then in the mount of Lebanon; now and at night-time wandering in the street, now in the wilderness, now in the garden, now in the fields, now in the house. Sometimes she is left desolate; sometimes she seeks and does not find; she calls, and He does not answer. Then again she rejoices because she hears the voice of the Beloved, and is assured of His never-changing faithfulness. At times she is deeply conscious of her unworthiness, and takes to heart the bitter reproaches of the watchmen; at other times the loyal spirit bursts forth in exultation, and she is persuaded that she is the chosen one, beautiful in His sight. The Song of Solomon describes, therefore, the experience of the pilgrim state; and though there are in this book Old Testament aspects which perhaps will be fully understood only when Israel is converted and restored, and though since the Incarnation and the gift of the Holy Ghost we have received deeper and fuller disclosures, yet is this Song a most precious and fragrant divinely-inspired commentary on this word: "Draw nigh to God, and He will draw nigh to you."

And you who feel that knowledge has puffed you up, and that love — humble, contrite, meek, and adoring love — has forsaken your heart, beware of two evils. Do not underrate the danger of your present state. Read the Lord's estimate of lukewarmness in His epistle to the Laodiceans. (Rev. iii.) Do not fall into despondency; for to you the loving Saviour addresses His most tender, compassionate, and touching words: "Behold, I stand at the door, and knock: if any man hear my voice, and open the door, I will come in to him, and will sup with him, and he with Me." If any Christian has gone astray, if the heart has become cold and dead, draw nigh to God. Oh, you who are weary of wandering from your God, and are now made willing to return, say to Jesus —

"Thou knowest the way to bring me back,
   My fallen spirit to restore;
Oh, for Thy truth and mercy's sake,
   Forgive, and bid me sin no more!
The ruins of my soul repair,
And make my heart a house of prayer."

Draw nigh to God, you who seek to draw others unto God — you parents and masters, who wish to be a blessing to your children and households — you teachers and evangelists and visitors, who seek the good of souls. Have you not felt a painful void after speaking for Christ, or doing something in His name, even though you spoke and acted in faith and prayer? The soul coming back to itself feels empty and exhausted. Power and blessing have gone out from you, but have you yourself been enriched and strengthened? ... "Draw nigh to God!" There is no place so good, so safe, so sweet for the teacher as the place of the learner — as the place of Mary, sitting at the Master's feet; as the place of Paul, bowing his knees before the God and Father of our Lord Jesus Christ!

There let us all unite and meet. Here on earth, amid all the noise and conflict, the sorrow and the trial of our pilgrimage; there, in glory, where we shall see Jesus as He is, and be for ever with Him, beholding, adoring, and serving His and our Father.

[1] I Cor. ii. 6, 7.

[2] Ps. li. 6.

[3] 2 John ii. 27.

[4] Job xxviii. 12, 14.

[5] Matt. xi. 25.

[6] The glory of the Lord shall be revealed. (Isa. xl. 5.)

[7] John ii. II.

[8] John xi. 4, 40.

[9] 2 Cor. iii.

[10] Phil. iii. 10.

[11] Rom. viii. 17.

[12] Col. iii. 3.

[13] John iii. 8.

[14] Gal. ii. 20.

[15] Rev. xix. 7, 9.

[16] John iv. 32.

[17] Ps. xlvi, 4; Rev. xxii. I.

[18] Especially the doctrine of grace, held to be fundamental in evangelical churches, has a mystical character; for it maintains that grace, and not nature, is the source of all our good thoughts, words, and works. "If I could obey in all things, yet that would not satisfy me, unless I felt obedience flow from the birth of His life in me. 'My Father doeth all things in Me,' saith Christ. This was Christ's comfort; and to feel Christ do all in the soul, is the comfort of one that truly believeth on Him."

[19] ROTHE, *Prediglen*, vol. iii. p. 213.

[20] John xv. 16; Jer. xxi. 3; 2 Cor. v. 18; i Cor. i. 30; Rom. ix. 16.

[21] In the parable of the prodigal, the repentance of the son is represented in its *manifestation*. He came to himself, he said, he willed, he arose. The secret source of this repentance is not mentioned — the mysterious drawing of the Father, and the influence of the Holy Ghost. The pedagogic wisdom of this silence is easily discerned.

[22] The following remarks are from an American author: "The soul only, when divinely influenced, receives its

power. Our faculties, like the eye that must be filled with light from without, wait for their power from above. It is the divine energy, acting through the human faculty, that gives to man his real existence. Nor does any man know his power, his nature, his richness of emotion, the height and depth of his being, until he unfolds under the influence of the Spirit of the living God. "That we are bound to God is as great a restriction of our liberty, as it is to a plant's freedom to be held by the sun."

[23] It is to be noticed that among all the "excuses" mentioned in our Lord's parable of the supper, the modern one of doubt, whether "the invitation is really meant for me," does not occur. They all felt they were invited to a supper, and were wished to come. And is not this what all who hear the gospel really feel below the artificial surface of half-digested doctrine?

[24] Dr. D. Brown.

[25] Calvin.

Note On Mystics

Indian and Mohammedan mystics contain many surprising glimpses of the highest truth. The deep desire and thirst of the human heart after the Eternal Origin and Fountain, expresses itself in their words with singular force and beauty. What can be more profound than the description of God-given, God-wrought prayer, in the lines on a Mohammedan saint:

"This prayer is not his own: God Himself is speaking.
See, God prays in him, and he stands in deep contemplation.
God has given him both the contemplation and the answer? [1]

There is truth and error in the remark of Schopenhauer on Christian and Indian 'penitents': "We are greatly struck by their similarity. With an utter dissimilarity of dogmas, customs, and external circumstances, their aspirations and inner life are identical. Quietism, or renunciation of all will; askesis, or voluntary mortifying of the self-will; and mysticism, or the recognition of the identity with the all or the root of the universe; these stand in closest connection." The Christian knows not only wherein religion consists, but he also knows the *source and power* of the true life. The mystics outside Christianity have truly felt the necessity of *death,* of hating our own will and life, and in this respect put to shame many professing Christians who mind earthly things, and are the enemies of the cross of Christ. But they did not know: "Ye have died *with Christ,* and your life is hid with Christ in God." They did not know the power of Christ's resurrection, and the constraining love of the Divine Saviour, who for us died and lived again, that we henceforth may live unto Him. They may therefore be viewed as resembling those who, through the law, have become dead and long for life.

The dangerous *tendencies* of Christian mystics (I use no stronger expression, because I do not think the more important and best-known of these writers have fallen into errors) seem to be (i) towards Pantheism. They dwell much on the Scriptural truth, that all things are of God and through Him and

16

to Him. They love to contemplate the union between God and man, between Christ and the believer — a union real and essential, and not merely ethical. It is here that they sometimes use unguarded expressions, of our being En-goded (vergottet) — "God so unites Himself with the soul, that they become one Spirit, one Substance" (Makarius) — and terms still more vague and misleading. Yet this ought not to prevent our appreciating their testimony of the truth of the indwelling of God in us, and our indwelling in Him.

2. They do not sufficiently distinguish between *Christ for us* and *Christ in us*. Even the best of this school, like Tersteegen, cannot state clearly the distinction between justification and sanctification; and a teacher so enlightened as Tauler, says, that as long as we are on earth we cannot attain to assurance of our acceptance and salvation.

3. They tend to divert the attention from Christ to the soul, in which God and Christ dwell; so that self (renewed and God-influenced, yet self) becomes the object of contemplation. This tendency is subtle, attractive, and dangerous. "I have a suspicion about the mystics," says Theremin; "they never are in a peculiar state of mind, but they immediately reflect on it and describe it." There is, contrary to their own theory, much of their own willing in their states and phases. To contemplate what Christ effects in us, instead of what Christ *is* — to dwell on what He has given us, instead of the unsearchable riches and fulness of the Lord — will produce *self-deception* instead of *self-judgment*, and can only *lower* the standard of Perfectness, which is none other but Christ Himself.

Our great and constant desire ought to be to know Christ, and, having no confidence in the flesh, to rejoice in Him, waiting for His coming, when, delivered from the body of sin, we shall be like Him. The constant watching of the growth of the inner man leads us also "to mistake passing emotions for real and abiding love of good," and to exalt any peculiar intuition into a source of self-glorification.

4. The relation of the inward teaching of the Spirit to the Scripture is sometimes not properly maintained. It is not clearly held that the Scripture-revelation and the direct teaching of the Spirit always go together, and that all inner experiences, intuitions, &c., must be judged by the written Word.

5. The objection most frequently urged, that they encourage a morbid quietism, a merely passive and receptive attitude, is true only in a limited degree. The mystics were driven into solitude by the mechanical and unspiritual externalism of works which surrounded them. This evil is not confined to any period or church. It is always man's tendency to work and speak and run, whether sent or not, and whether or not 'the hour is come.' Against this the mystics protested; but that they did not encourage false quietism may be seen from such passages as the following, from Tauler: "The righteous exercise themselves inwardly and outwardly; they endure in all paths into which God leads them, in temptation and in darkness, and do not pretend that they have already reached the state of quietude. Works of love are more pleasing

to God than great contemplativeness. If thou art in spiritual devotion, and God sends thee to go out to preach or to serve a sick brother, God will be more present to thee than if thou remainest in secret contemplation."

The mystic writers will always be a useful protest against the mere 'form of godliness,' and the letter that killeth; but the minds that feel most attracted by them need most to be on their guard in reading them. Let everything lead us to the spiritual and diligent study of the perfect, healthful, and precious *word of God*.

[1] Quoted by Tholuck on Rom. viii. 26: "The Spirit maketh intercession for us."

Chapter Two - Sincerity in Drawing Nigh to God

"Draw nigh to God, and He will draw nigh to you." - James iv. 8.

ALTHOUGH man has forsaken God, the fountain of living water, he has not given up the desire for something to satisfy the thirst of his spirit. He seeks light for the mind, love for the heart, peace for the soul; he seeks honour and glory. He is not content with existence; he wishes to live; he wants fulness of life, vigorous, joyous, long-enduring. He still wants water, though he has left God. This it is which he seeks in broken cisterns. And yet God is the only fountain of living water. Have we returned to Him? Have we found Him whom ignorantly we were seeking? Have we become the disciples and children of the heavenly wisdom? and is our inward eye rejoicing now in the light, so that we can say, It is pleasant to behold the sun? Have we, as weary and heavy-laden ones, come to Jesus, and has He given us the blood-purchased, perfect peace? Have we found the only One who is worthy to be loved with the whole heart, and has divine love been shed abroad by the Holy Ghost? Are we seeking the only true honour which Cometh from God? as Jesus said, "If any man serve Me, him will my Father honour." Are we on our way to heaven — drawing nigh to God? Then do we rejoice with joy unspeakable and full of glory, a solemn, humble, heaven-anticipating joy —

"I've found the pearl of greatest price;
    My heart doth sing for joy.
 Christ Jesus is the heaven of heaven,
    My Christ, what shall I call?
 Christ is the first, Christ is the last,
    And Christ is all in all."

It is a great thing to have found Christ. Once He was nothing to us; then He became something to us; but now He is all to us. It is a great thing that those who have found Christ abide in Him, even as it will be a great thing to be glorified together with Him. As it is great, it needs all our thought and purpose, diligence and watchfulness; it is the one thing we do, we are busy in "our salvation," and this with fear and trembling. As it is glorious, so, alas! there are many counterfeits, many deceivers, many self-deceived. Many who look like sheep on the hill-side are seen by God to be dead stones. Some (so the Saviour warns us) who say emphatically and sweetly, Lord, are strangers to Jesus; He never knew them. Many who are busy and troubled about many things in the service of Christ have never yet chosen the one thing needful, the good part which shall not be taken from us.

It has been remarked [1] that a hypocrite generally thinks himself the sincerest person in the world. The godly, in whose spirit there is no guile, examine themselves, distrust their deceitful hearts, and pray to God: "Search me, and know my heart; try me, and know my thoughts." [2]

The Scripture warnings are very solemn, but only drive us to Him who will never deceive us, and who will not withhold anything that is good from them that are upright in heart. Searcher of hearts, I feel only safe with thee; and the more I know thee as the Searcher of hearts, the more I love thee as the Healer of hearts. Eyes of Jesus, like a flame of fire, when you wound the heart, the unfaithful disciple goes out and weeps bitterly. Bright light of God's throne, I cannot approach thee while I conceal my sin, and while unloving thoughts toward my brother fill my soul; but if I walk in the light, and have fellowship with my brethren, the blood of Jesus Christ, God's Son, cleanseth me from all sin.

What is meant by sincerity in drawing nigh to God?

This question is suggested by the text itself, and by the words which immediately follow, and which are addressed to the double-minded. A most forcible expression (δίψυχοι), reminding us of the Psalmist's, "A heart and a heart. [3] James is most valuable as a teacher, helping us to a knowledge of sin, and yet his pen is steeped in grace." [4] Continuing the Master's testimony against the Pharisees, he exhorts us to have the faith of our Lord in singleness of heart, thought, speech, and action.

Thus in the first chapter he speaks of singleness of heart toward God, who giveth in simplicity (ἁπλῶς), and who is simple and unmixed light. In the second chapter he exhorts us to have the faith in our Lord in simplicity, without respect to persons. He also shows us the unity of the law; it is one, .and undivided. In the third chapter he insists on simplicity in speech, that we should bless God and men, which are made in the similitude of God. In the fourth chapter he warns us against a double heart in our communion with God. The whole epistle is a comment on the petition of David, "Unite my heart," and of the word of the Lord, "If thine eye be single, thy whole body will be full of light."

When we speak of drawing nigh to God, we think immediately of prayer, and yet prayer is only one manifestation of drawing nigh to God. True it is the most important, concentrated, and, so to say, the culminating point of the soul's approach to God, We may say, that as our prayer so is our life. Our prayer is what God hears, not merely the words we utter; God hears our thoughts, the desires of our hearts.

We may also say, that as our life is, so is our prayer, into which it returns, and in which it expresses itself. Behold one approaching the altar of God. He draws nigh to God; so it appears to himself, so it appears to us. But the last week's or month's life has left a bitter sediment in his heart. His brother has something against him. There is a cloud of hatred, or estrangement, or envy, or injustice between him and his brother. Can he, does he, draw nigh to God? When Jesus says, "If ye forgive not men their trespasses, neither will your Father forgive your trespasses," He announces a principle, of which this one particular sin is only an illustration. There is a prayer which is not prayer; there is a false and fruitless drawing near to God, and this is its character — insincerity; or as the psalmist says: "If I regard iniquity in my heart, the Lord will not hear me.

Sin is that which separates between God and us. His ear is not heavy, that it cannot hear, and His hand is not shortened, that it cannot save. He delighteth in mercy: it is His joy to bless; it is His glory to heal and to comfort. But we must draw near with a true heart. It may be asked: Is not Jesus the propitiation for our sins? and are we not to draw nigh to God just as we are? Let us examine this point more closely.

God redeemed Israel by the blood of the Lamb, that they might serve Him. They knew what they worshipped. They adored the living God, the Fountain of blessedness, holy, just, and true. They knew His mercy, and the way of access unto His throne. God appointed the way in which they were to 'draw nigh.' The light may have been but dim, but it was true and God-given. They knew God, a just God, and yet a Saviour. And yet of this people, thus approaching God in the way He had appointed, and offering the sacrifices which God had ordained, the Lord complains: "This people draweth near unto Me with their lips, but their hearts are far from Me." "To what purpose is the multitude of your sacrifices unto Me."... Wash you, make you clean; put away the evil of your doings from before mine eyes; cease to do evil; learn to do well." Strange language, when we think that not by works, but by grace we are saved, and that the sacrifices spoken of were types of the only sacrifice and substitute, without whose shed blood is no remission of sin. To translate this language into the language of the New Testament times, it would be thus: To what purpose is the multitude of your appeals to Jesus, as your perfect Righteousness, and your prayers in the name of Him, who came to save you from your sins? Cleanse your hands, ye sinners, and purify your hearts, ye double-minded. "Draw nigh to God, and He will draw nigh to you."

"Come now, and let us reason together, saith the Lord: though your sins be as scarlet, they shall be as white as snow; though they be red like crimson, they shall be as wool." This verse is often quoted to encourage the sinner to turn to God. It doubtless contains one of the most comforting declarations of the wonderful mercy of God. It is addressed to the chief of sinners, and speaks of grace abounding. But is it right and safe to separate this word from the context? Is it right to forget the *now* which connects the appeal with the preceding command, "Wash you, make you clean"? or to sever it from the exposure of formalism, insincerity, and hypocrisy which goes before this exhortation? Are we to preach the gospel differently from prophets and apostles? or are we afraid that the message will lose its power and sweetness when we give it fully? This be far from us!

The difficulty may arise, however, that there is a contradiction here to the truth of free grace. Does the prophet mean that we must *first* cleanse ourselves from evil before we draw nigh to God, and that then God will forgive and receive us? No; he declares the glad tidings of salvation and of free pardon, or, in New Testament language, Jesus receiveth sinners. But sinners who wish to come to God, who not merely wish to be rescued out of danger and delivered from pain, but whose desire is to be received of God, to be assured of His love, to be renewed by His Spirit, to turn from sin to God, from earth to heaven, from self to Christ. If we draw nigh to God, if in Jesus we approach Him, He will immediately receive, He will abundantly pardon.

Unless this truth be fully stated, men may be dealing with shadows instead of realities; they may never realize what is meant by God, by sin, by reconciliation; they may deceive themselves with the most fatal delusion and dream of divine love, which they have never experienced in its awful holiness and in its fatherly sweetness.

It is strange, that what would be immediately granted to be true in the case of very flagrant vice, is only reluctantly acknowledged to apply to all men and to all sin. What is the gospel I am to preach to one addicted to some vice? Am I to say to him, You must first give up your evil habit, and then draw nigh to God? This would be extremely wrong, foolish, cruel. Reminding him of what sin is, how evil, dishonouring to God, and ruinous to man; what a power and tyranny, we must speak of the love of God, the blood of Christ, and the renewing grace of the Saviour. But is it not part of the message, that he must turn to God with the full and sincere resolution to give up his sinful habit? I may say to him. Do not be astonished if you find it still difficult, even after your conversion to God, to give up this sin; do not feel despair if you should have most painful struggle and occasional failure, but God will help you, only turn to Him, surrendering your whole will to *His* will, who has said, No drunkard, &c., shall inherit the kingdom of God,

If this is true of drunkenness, of lying, of stealing, is it not true of every sin? And does not drawing nigh to God — faith in Jesus — imply the full and sincere determination of departing from all iniquity? Can there be a real transaction between God and the soul, can there be a real beholding of Jesus and His death on the cross, without this inward and painful turning away from sin?

There are two elements, inseparably connected by God, which when separated change their character. God is *holy* and *righteous* Love, and He desires truth and purity in us. God is *merciful* and *gracious* Love, and He receives sinners freely in Christ, Now when the message is brought. Draw nigh to God, some who are impressed with the holy and righteous character of God, interpret the call to mean that they must amend their lives, and, if possible, purify their hearts. Others seem to understand the free invitation and the immediate acceptance of the sinner through Christ, but they do not see the necessary connection between this grace and the renewal of the heart, the transformation of their character, the turning round from sin to the service of God. Now both, although taking hold of opposite poles of truth, make the same mistake. They do not realize the *living God;* they do not behold Jesus Himself, and Him crucified.

To turn away from sin, and to behold the mercy of God in Christ, is repentance unto life. Some are sincere in wishing to be delivered from sin, but they do not turn to *God.* Some fancy they have come to God, but they have never turned away from *sin.* [5] It is true, we are to come with all our sins; but we are to come with them *against* them to condemn them before God, and declare ourselves determined to forsake them, that He may deliver us from them all. It is true, that only by drawing nigh to God can we obtain the forgiveness of sin and the victory over sin. But we cannot ask the one without desiring the other. We cannot be gladdened by the light of Christ's resurrection, except we have our heart broken on account of sin and from sin by looking at the Lamb of God crucified for us. We cannot be admitted into the kingdom unless we die to sin and to the world. This strait gate, this new birth, this rending of the heart, this death-blow to the old man, is indispensable. Jesus is not the servant of sin, but the Saviour of sinners. He takes away the false peace of a self-satisfied heart, and heals the broken-hearted. [6]

Without this there is no drawing nigh to God. To be consciously in the presence of God and of the Lamb, to approach spiritually the mercy-seat, involves the reception of the twofold truth: Jesus died for me; Jesus is henceforth to dwell and live in me. Unless we realize both these truths, we do not realize God; and Jesus may say to us, "Hitherto ye have asked nothing in my name." For *what* is it that such imaginary coming to Jesus asks of Him, but to be allowed to retain the false comfort of peace when there is no peace. There is no other real petition offered, either for light, or love, or strength, to serve God and to glorify His name.

It was said by the angel concerning Saul of Tarsus, after the Lord had appeared unto him, "Behold, he prayeth." Saul had no doubt been in the habit of praying from his childhood; and without charging him with hypocrisy or formalism, it is evident that in the true and full sense of the word he had never prayed to God until Jesus had appeared unto him. What was the difference between his former prayers and his present approach? for as a Pharisee he had prayed to the true and living God. The difference was this. Formerly he approached, having his own righteousness. As he felt it sufficient, he drew near with an imperfect thing to the Perfect One, and therefore, unconsciously but most really, he lowered God in his idea, and brought Him down to his own level.

In the presence of such a conception of God, sin does not appear exceeding sinful, and no cry of true petition ascends out of the depth. And as there is no crucifixion of the old man, there is no birth of the new, no resurrection-life and power. Such prayer leaves the 'self-righteous as he was before. But when Jesus appeared to Saul, then he beheld his whole past life as sinful, his righteousness as filthy rags, his zeal as zeal against God; the name of the Lord as Jesus, Saviour, deepened still further the agonizing sense of his guilt. Now he was no longer heart-whole; his righteousness and his peace vanished; he stood before God a sinner. He cried out of the depths, he turned with loathing from the things of which he formerly boasted, and hid himself in Jesus. Now it became clear to him what Jehovah meant by always speaking of *His* righteousness, of His salvation; now he understood that not by the works of the law, but by the grace of the Lord, can Abraham's seed be justified.

Thus when we really draw nigh to *God,* we must take hold of Christ, and submit ourselves to the righteousness of God, which is in Him. When we have a view of the perfection of God; when we understand in our heart, to some extent, the holy name of the Saviour-God, Jehovah, then we joyfully accept the declaration of grace: Jehovah-Tsidkenu — the Lord our Righteousness. It is because men do not see God that they do not feel the need of mediation. When in the presence of God, we cannot abide without the best robe, without righteousness, divine, perfect, all-glorious; whiter than snow, whiter than any fuller, whiter than any earthly art or skill can make it. Like the light of the sun, the righteousness of God falls on us, and in Christ Jesus we are made the righteousness of God.

When we thus accept Christ for us, the Son of God is revealed *in us.* (Gal. i. 16.)

By this very act of coming to Jesus, we are separated from sin. The same hand which blots out our sins, writes the law of God on our hearts. The new man is born, the old man is nailed to the cross. As we condemn ourselves, both our so-called good works and our sin— ourselves the guilty and polluted branches of the first Adam — so we are transplanted into the kingdom of God, grafted into Christ, that He may now live in us. Paul felt now that Christ, who was his Righteousness, was his Master and Lord, his guide and joy, his life and strength; and that as Jesus had identified Himself with Stephen, so now he would identify Himself with him. Paul is therefore, indeed, a new creature; he is reconciled to God, he is in Christ. This is conversion. The sinner, feeling the burden of sin, cries to God, Have mercy upon *me,* O *God!* And as the sinner seeks God, so God seeks the sinner, his heart, the surrender of the whole man — the salvation and future glory of the lost one, for whom Jesus died. Thus God finds the sinner, and rejoices; the sinner finds God, and is at peace.

"Less than Thyself will not suffice
  My comfort to restore.
A sense of Thine expiring love
  Into my soul convey;
Thyself bestow; for Thee alone
  I absolutely pray."

Our blessed Lord, who is Himself both the great Evangelist and the great Gospel, while never discouraging sinners who draw near to hear Him, always discouraged those who wished to substitute a mere outward reception of His truth for the real inward turning from sin unto God. When the multitudes came to listen to His teaching He did not regard this as an infallible sign of their right condition, or give them an immediate assurance of their safety; but He showed, in the parable of the sower, what was the character of true hearing. When men enthusiastically offered their allegiance, Jesus put before them all the difficulties and severe conditions of discipleship, that man must deny himself, and take up his cross; that unless we prefer Christ to father and mother and to our own life, we are not worthy of Him. Yet is Jesus the Saviour, who will not break the bruised reed, nor quench the smoking flax; yet is it God, who Himself works in us both to will and to do.

Jesus is the great magnet. When the soul is drawn by Him, and approaches God in Christ, there is the twofold experience, bitter and sweet; the experience of death, painful and humiliating, the experience of life, joyous and full of consolation and peace. The sword of the law goes again through our soul more piercing than ever, while the kiss of the Father heals and gladdens our heart.

In a recent poem [7] this experience is described very forcibly, only that it is erroneously represented to take place after the soul's departure from this life. Beholding the Lord in His holy and merciful love, the soul feels pierced with an overwhelming sense of sin and guilt, and at the same time blessed with the sweet hope of ineffable grace. The guardian angel thus describes the twofold effect of the approach to the Saviour:

        "...Praise to His name!
The eager spirit has departed from my hold.
And, with the intemperate energy of love,
Flies to the dear feet of Emmanuel;
But, ere it reach them, the keen sanctity,
Which with its effluence, like a glory, clothes
And circles round the Crucified, has seized,
And scorched, and shrivelled it; and now it lies
Passive and still before the awful Throne.
O happy, suffering soul! for it is safe,
Consumed, yet quickened, by the glance of God."

This is what happens *on earth,* when we are brought by the Spirit to look unto Him whom we have pierced, and to mourn. As Newton described it —

"In evil long I took delight,
　　Unawed by shame or fear.
　Till a new object struck my sight,
　　And stopped my wild career.

"I saw One hanging on a tree.
　　In agonies and blood.
　Who fixed His languid eyes on me.
　　As near His cross I stood.

"Sure never till my latest breath
　　Can I forget that look;
　It seemed to charge me with His death.
　　Though not a word He spoke.

"My conscience felt and owned the guilt,
　　And plunged me in despair;
　I saw my sins His blood had spilt,
　　And helped to nail Him there.

"Alas! I knew not what I did;
　　But now my tears are vain;
　Where shall my trembling soul be hid?
　　For I the Lord have slain.

"A second look He gave, which said,
　　'I freely all forgive;
　This blood is for thy ransom paid;
　　I die that thou may'st live.'

"Thus, while His death my sin displays
　　In all its blackest hue,
　(Such is the mystery of grace)
　　It seals my pardon too.

"With pleasing grief and mournful joy
　　My spirit now is filled,
　That I should such a life destroy,
　　Yet live by Him I killed."

This is conversion, and here is the source of our holiness.

Thus coming unto God, from one and the same central transaction flow justification and sanctification, distinct but inseparable. If conversion is truly understood, and has really taken place, no new starting-point is needed for sanctification. When the apostles answers indignantly the false accusation inferred from his doctrine of justification by faith, he does not need to add anything to that doctrine, but only to repeat it, to show what is most unmistakeably and fully involved in it. How can we live unto sin, seeing that by coming unto Jesus, crucified for us, we have died unto sin? How can we sin, seeing that we are not under the law, which condemns and gives no life, but under grace, which brings to us both the pardon and the power of God, because it brings *God* to us, and us to *God?* [8]

How much does the Christian need to be reminded of sincerity in prayer! It is easy to mistake passing emotions for that abiding and true faith which worketh in love, and to rest in our admiration of intense and spiritual petitions which have not yet become the desire of the heart and the concentrated determination of the will. There is often one idol, one cherished sin, of which we are conscious, but which we are not willing to bring into the light of the countenance, the thorn -crowned countenance, before which sin cannot remain uncondemned. There may be one habit, if not of sin in the ordinary sense of the word, yet of that which is not of faith. [9] It is from such concealment and insincerity that the mists of darkness rise, the clouds which obstruct the light and keep us without joy and strength.

And while in this state, let us not deceive ourselves with "objective religion," or looking away from self. McCheyne said, "that for one look at self we ought to take ten looks at Christ." Excellent counsel of a true Israelite, in whom was no guile! But we cannot do without that *one* look at our heart, at our ways. He who does not come to *himself* will not go to the Father. Can we ever say, "Bless the Lord," if we have never said, "O my soul"?

But we who have tasted that the Lord is gracious can draw near boldly, pouring out all our heart before the throne of grace. We know that it is not merely solemn, but blessed, to confess our sin. [10] We pray for sincerity; and mourning over our insincerity, we bring to God the broken and contrite heart which He will not despise.

II. As we turn from sin, so we turn also from *worldliness*. Christ has delivered us from this present evil age; the love of the Father from the love of the world. When we think of the birth and the consummation of our new life, this becomes very clear.

The hidden life has its root and birth in *death*. "Ye have died with Christ, and your life is hid with Christ in God." "I have been crucified with Christ: but I live; yet not I, Christ liveth in me." The hidden life has its consummation and crown in the *second advent* of our Lord: "When Christ, who is our life, shall appear, then shall ye also appear with Him in glory." The boundary-lines of this blessed land are therefore the cross of the Lord Jesus and the return of the Bridegroom. Do you think that, with such a starting-point as baptism into the Saviour's death, and with such a goal as the marriage supper of the Lamb, Christians can love the world and the things of the world?

"Draw nigh to God." The call implies not merely a turning away from sin, but also from the world. Only they who have the mind of strangers and pilgrims can expect to have fellowship with Jesus. "They are not of the world, even as I am not of the world." It is in the wilderness, and not in Egypt, that the Lord guides His people. The garden into which the Beloved enters is that holy garden, planned by eternal love, and prepared by redeeming grace, by Christ and the Holy Ghost. If led captive into Babylon, the Lord will comfort all who mourn and hang their harps on the willows; but He is far from all who forget Jerusalem, and feel at home by Babel's streams. The Bridegroom is with the chaste virgin, who goes forth to meet Him. The narrow path, commencing with the cross — "Ye have died with Christ" — ending with the glory of Jesus, is the path on which the Lord draws near and walks with His disciples.

All the epistles describe this experience. There may be difference of opinion as to apostolic doctrines, but there can be no doubt as to the nature of Christian life and experience; that the believer is separated from sin in his inmost soul, and by the very love which redeemed him and brought unto him complete and everlasting forgiveness; that the believer is one with Jesus, and that, by faith in Christ's death, he has consigned the old man, with his affections and lusts, to death, even the cross; that his citizenship is now in heaven; that he is dead unto the world, and has his affection set upon things above; and that he looks forward constantly unto the return of the Master, Of this all the apostolic epistles testify in terms most unmistakeable. I can imagine a candid reader of the New Testament object, that such a character as the Christian must needs be melancholy. The critic might easily object, that such men as Christians are described to be, would not be fit for the work and not inclined for the amusements of the world; that they would be useless to the State; that they would take no interest in war, or in politics, or in commerce, or in literature and art. Such objections, though erroneous, would be quite natural. And if people were more honest, and did not take it for granted that they are, and must be regarded as, Christians, such objections would be more frequently raised. We have not laid sufficient stress on the unworldly or otherworldly character of the Christian's present life. "The time is short," or, as the original means, the time is shortened, the respite limited, the coming of the Lord draweth nigh. "It remaineth that both they that have wives be as though they had none; and they that weep, as though they wept not; and they that rejoice, as though they rejoiced not; and they that buy, as though they possessed not; and they that use this world, as not abusing it; for the fashion of this world passeth away."

But the Christian is called to live in the world, [11] to let his light shine before men, to adorn the doctrine of the gospel in whatever calling he is placed. He is exhorted to look upon the world as the field where the seed of the gospel is to be sown, where the character of Jesus is to be manifested by His followers, and where God is to be glorified. He is to conquer by faith and love. He is to be a prophet, priest, and king, teaching truth and righteousness, proclaiming peace, and offering intercession, living in a royal spirit above the distractions and anxieties of time. He can be a missionary everywhere: Christ sends him into the world. He can attain to the dignity of a confessor and martyr, though in humility and meekness he does not seek to rouse opposition, but to commend himself to the conscience of all. The less he loves the world in its God-opposed character, the more he truly loves the world, and is a blessing to those around him.

Turning from worldliness, we do not turn to a life of inactivity, but to a life of service. What wilt thou have me to *do?* is the question of the Christ-called man. The Thessalonians turned from idols to *serve* the living God. We are emancipated from the fetters of sin and the world, we are transplanted into the kingdom of God, to work in the love and energy of our renewed heart. *He* labours most abundantly who realizes most fully that he is a stranger and pilgrim on earth, that he is not a citizen of time, but that eternity is his home, that God is his portion.

Let all whose hearts are toward the Lord magnify Him, and rejoice in God their Saviour. Lift up your eyes from your sin and misery to the God and Father of our Lord Jesus Christ. Behold the *manner* of divine love, that it is fatherly! See it in its motherly tenderness, intensity, and constant solicitude. Rise to the exalted and confiding dignity of friendship, to which Jesus the Son of God has called you. Go forth with all the saved and sanctified to meet, with solemn joy and hope, the Bridegroom. He who made you sorry after a godly sort, is the source of your joy. Rejoice, and be glad in Him. Then you will say:

"My whole desire doth deeply turn away
  Out of all time unto eternal day.
  I give myself, and all I call my own,
  To Christ for ever, to be His alone." [12]

Until at last we reach our home —

"Then long Eternity shall greet our bliss
  With an individual kiss,
  And joy shall overtake us as a flood,
  When everything that is sincerely good
  And perfectly divine
  With truth, and peace, and love, shall ever shine
  About the supreme throne
  Of Him, to whose happy-making sight alone,
  When once our heav'nly-guided soul shall climb.
  Then all this earthly grossness quit,
  Attir'd with stars, we shall for ever sit
  Triumphing over Death and Chance and thee, O Time." [13]

[1] Kohlbrügge.
[2] "The godly man hates the evil he possibly by temptation hath been drawn to do, and loves the good he is frustrated of, and, having intended, hath not attained to do. The sinner, who hath his denomination from sin as his course, hates the

good which sometimes he is forced to do, and loves that sin which many times he does not, either wanting occasion and means, so that he cannot do it, or through the check of an enlightened conscience possibly dares not do; and though so bound up from the act, as a dog in a chain, yet the habit, the natural inclination and desire in him, is still the same, the strength of his affection is carried to sin. So in the weakest sincere Christian, there is that predominant sincerity and desire of holy walking, according to which he is called a righteous person: the Lord is pleased to give him that name, and account him so, being upright in heart though often failing." — Archbishop Leighton.

[3] Psalm xii. 2: "Flattering lips and a double heart."

[4] Nitzsch.

[5] The prophets contain many illustrations of this self-deception; for instance, Zech. vii. 5: "Speak unto all the people of the land, and to the priests, saying, When ye fasted and mourned in the fifth and seventh month, even those seventy years, did ye at all fast unto me, even to me?" The frequent exhortations in Isaiah and Jeremiah, point out that false repentance does not go deep enough — the turning from sin; and not high enough — turning to God. While the epistles are profitable and applicable to the true Church, the kernel of the congregation, the *prophets* are most needed by the actual mixed congregation of gospel-hearers and professing Christians.

[6] We come to Jesus 'just as we are;' yet not to remain 'just as we are,' but to be washed, renewed, and set apart for God's service.

[7] J. H. Newman, *Dream of Gerontius*.

[8] So in the first epistle of John, from another point of view. You have come to Jesus, you are born of God; you cannot sin, because the seed of God abideth in you.

[9] "There is very much of *suspense of conscience* among Christians upon subjects of practical life, upon which there is no suspense of *action*."— Phelps.

[10] Nitzsch, with his peculiar conciseness and depth, says of confession of sin: "Nothing is so truly an action, and a suffering, and a decision of the will, as confessing our sin to God."

[11] Compare my work, *Christ and the Church*, chap. vii.

[12] Tersteegen.

[13] Milton, *Ode to Time*.

Chapter Three - Encouragements to Prayer

I have endeavoured to explain what is meant by drawing nigh unto God. Beholding the two inseparable gifts which the exalted Saviour holds in His pierced hand, repentance and faith, we have seen what is meant by sincerity in drawing nigh to God, a true turning away from sin and worldliness unto the grace and love and life of God, which in a crucified and risen Saviour are freely given to us. Let us now dwell on the abundant mercy, the overflowing riches, the infinite love, awaiting us when we draw nigh; the atmosphere of free and all-sufficient grace which we breathe when we approach the God and Father of our Lord Jesus Christ. All divine revelations encourage us to draw nigh to God.

It is man's duty to draw nigh to God. Reason and conscience fully admit this. The first commandment, and the foundation of all other command-ments, is to worship God. But it is only in times of great and grievous dulness that the believer regards prayer as a duty, and not as a privilege. What higher dignity, what greater and more precious gift could we possibly possess? [1] "Behold, what manner of love the Father hath bestowed upon us."

In every place, and at all times, we may come into His presence. In the name of Jesus we appear before His throne of grace, and He beholds us in Him, and loves us as His children. Though we cannot express in words what our souls desire and long for, we know that He interprets and hears the lan-guage of our heart. To Him we may confide what we could intrust to no hu-man friend; where all earthly help is of no avail, we can ask His almighty suc-cour. The thoughts and doubts which rise within us we can spread out before Him, to sift, to correct, to change them; the sorrow that lies too deep for hu-man ministry we can bring to Love, omnipotent and all-compassionate. And we know that we can never weary Him with our approach, and that not one thought or petition will be overlooked by Him; all good that we ask will be granted abundantly, and with overflowing and tender mercies. And this is not all. Had we no petitions to offer, no gifts, no consolations, no deliverances to ask, what a privilege is prayer, were it merely to stand before the Lord, to be in the presence of the Holy and Blessed One, to behold with open face His glory, and to know that He sees and loves us, and that, through the blood of Christ, we have been brought into the circle of eternal life — one with all an-gels and saints!

Still we often feel lassitude in prayer, and our hearts seem heavy, and not willing or able to rise into this serene and bright region. The Lord Jesus, the heavenly Wisdom and the true lover of men, counsels us always to pray, and not to faint. Is not our tendency always to faint, and not to pray? If we went to God with our cares and difficulties, with our sorrows and fears, aye, even with our apathy and sluggishness of mind and heart, we should obtain calm-ness, patience, strength. Instead of this, we go about weak, unhappy, with self-consuming care and self-reproach, in which there is no recuperative power. Our disinclination to pray is our most painful experience; it is so irra-tional and unaccountable. When we neglect prayer, a heavy weight is on our mind and heart; we anticipate, we exaggerate difficulties, we succumb to them; there is a cloud between us and our fellow-men; there is a cloud and veil between us and our heart; we have, as it were, lost it, even as we find our heart in approaching God.

"Prayer makes the darkened cloud withdraw;
Prayer climbs the ladder Jacob saw;
Gives exercise to faith and love,
Brings every blessing from above."

We are convinced of this; we have experienced it. [2] And yet how often we feel unwilling to pray, disinclined to go to Him who is all-glorious and all-good, who never receives us with harshness or indifference, who is always ready to bless, to comfort, and to help! Sometimes, even when we have abundance of leisure and solitude, when God in His providence seems to invite us to speak to Him, we feel this apathy. And yet we know that God regards even a look — hears even the desire of heart unuttered; that not even words are needful. Let us be deeply humbled, but let us not sink into despondency. Hear the voice: "Draw nigh to God!" Let us dwell frequently on the encouragements to draw nigh to God.

God draws; Satan only tempts. [3] All the evil influences which seek to prevent our approach to God do not deserve to be compared with the attractive power of God. I dare not speak lightly of the innate love of sin and the world, or of the tendency of fallen human hearts to gravitate to the earth, or of the force of habit, or of the fascinations of that enchanted ground, this present age, which lulls us to sleep, or of the subtilty and power of Satan. No; these are great and potent influences, but nothing when contrasted with God. Satan and all evil under and with him cannot prevail. Satan is powerful, but not omnipotent; he is cunning, but neither omniscient nor wise. He has an ally within us, even sin; but he has never yet understood a human heart. God alone can search the heart; He alone can draw it, can open, can melt, can fill it. Satan has no right, no claim on me, on my nature, on my will, on my affection. However wicked and polluted a human being may be, it is not his *nature* to be evil. And though he be so degraded as to feed the swine in the far country, that dark citizen has no real claim on him, and no true affinity with him. Man's heart was created for the love of God, and will only be happy there. The eye of his soul was made to behold the sun, and to rejoice in the light. And fallen though he be, his very misery proves his original grandeur. Let us remember that God created man in His image. Let us never forget that at the right hand of God is the man Christ Jesus. Let us behold ourselves, not in the wreck and ruin of our fallen condition, not in the mirror of the world and of Satan, but in the mirror of the hope of resurrection, when the purpose of God shall be fulfilled in us, and we shall be conformed to the image of His Son. When the transforming power of the precious blood of Christ shall be made manifest on the resurrection morn, there shall arise with transfigured and spiritual bodies, true human beings, full of love and truth, without a single spot, blemish, or wrinkle, holy and pure like Christ. If it be so, look upon evil as judged, condemned, and slain; upon Satan as bound and cast out. He cannot draw; he cannot reach the inmost depth of your self; he has no right over you; he has no power except the power you give him. Only resist, only show your face as conscious of your divine origin, only adore God, and Satan, powerless and abashed, will flee from you. There is no *real* connection between us and Satan. [4]

Oh, how different is it with God! He is the magnet. We are His offspring. He is able to *dwell* in us, and to make us dwell in Him. He draws with an irresistible power, and yet He does not force or compel us. He sets us free when His love subdues our heart. He restores us when He takes possession of our souls; for of Him and through Him and to Him are all things. He is our rightful Lord, He alone the King, whose it is to rule; and His rule is love.

And as to Satan, so to sin and the world, and all things of time and sense, you can say: Think not of holding me. I belong not to you; I no longer gravitate downward. Christ has redeemed me and rescued me, and lifted me up to Himself, and, like all angels and saints, heaven is my home, eternity is my element, God is my centre — I draw nigh to *God*. All in God *draws* me; everything within and around *drives* me to the throne of grace. I am ignorant, and know not what a day may bring forth. "How unsearchable are God's judgments, and His ways past finding out!" Shall I not draw nigh to infinite wisdom, to the great Sovereign, and say, "Guide me, O thou great Jehovah!" I am helpless; I cannot do that which is least; I cannot add an inch to my stature. Shall I not go to Him, without whose will not a sparrow can fall to the ground, who numbers the very hairs of my head, and ask Him to watch, defend, and strengthen me? Shall I not commit to Him every thing, great and small? I think of God's pity and compassion, of His bounteous liberality, of His joy and delight in giving and consoling, and shall I hesitate to ask, to pour out my complaints, to mourn before Him? I think of His fatherly omniscience, omnipotence, and love, and I lay before Him my sins, my failures, my disappointments and defeats in the fight of faith. I humble myself, and yet do not feel degraded; I confess my sins, and I know it will not alter or diminish His love to me, or cause Him to doubt me for the future, and to withhold from me His gifts. What earthly father would make an ungenerous use of the confidence of a child, and of his complaints over the evil he finds in his heart?

But our chief encouragement, the great and unanswerable argument, the bright light before which all shadows and doubts vanish, is the love of God in Christ Jesus. Who of us would ever have ventured to ask of God such a gift, such a sacrifice, as of His own spontaneous and infinite love He made in the sending of His own Son, and delivering Him up unto death? Could any creature have imagined such love, or been bold enough to supplicate such mercy? When God has thus given the best and greatest gift, when He spared not Him who was unspeakably more precious to Him than all finite creatures, how can we ever doubt His love to us. His delight in our salvation and blessedness?

All of the Godhead that can be known is manifested in Christ Jesus, and calls unto us, Draw nigh to God; for God has drawn nigh to you in love!

Jesus not merely reveals God, the hearer of prayer. He is also our Mediator. Jesus was a Man of prayer; He prayed without ceasing; and yet He had special seasons of drawing nigh unto His heavenly Father. The evangelist Luke, who dwells emphatically on the humanity of Christ, speaks frequently of the

Saviour's prayers. Twice we read of the Lord going out into a wilderness or solitary place, and twice into a mountain, to pray. We read of his continuing all night in prayer to God.

Jesus teaches us to pray. The Son of God knows the Father's heart, and what He is willing to grant; the Son of man knows the human heart, and what we need; and as He came to be not merely our Mediator, but our Head, He brings us into communion with Himself; so that we pray in His name, in unison with His intercession in our behalf, and in sympathy with His earthly experience. For when Jesus, in reply to the request, "Lord, teach us to pray," gave us the model prayer. He gave it out of His own constant experience. How did Jesus pray? He prayed to the Father in the full consciousness that He came from God, and was going again to His Father; in perfect trust and love; in the spirit of Sonship. He prayed as the Brother, in the spirit of fraternal and priestly love; He, who was always in heaven, realized the majesty, grandeur, riches, holiness, and power of the Father. He prayed in the royal and free spirit to the Father in heaven — our Father in heaven. Put your hand into Christ's hand, and your spirit, let it be folded within His. He is the only-begotten Son, and says, "Father;" you are adopted in Him, and the spirit of adoption within you says, "Father." He loved His own; He was full of love towards all; He had the Saviour-mind, the Shepherd-heart, towards all, especially towards them that believe. Then, like Him, say, *Our;* let your heart expand towards all you love, and the Church, and the world, and to the filial spirit add the fraternal. High above earth is the Source of all blessing, power, and peace, the Treasury which can never be exhausted — the glorious fulness and riches of God. Look up above all difficulties, sorrows, and wants of time, and doubt not that all is well, and all will end in perfection and peace. Now if Jesus has thus enabled me to say, *Father,* and *our,* and *in heaven,* I understand the seven petitions, and sympathise with them. Jesus came to declare the Father's name, to establish His kingdom, to redeem and restore earth. Is not this what I need? is not this that wherein God is glorified? So let me desire for myself, for the brethren, for all, the Name, the kingdom, the will of God, His Name is a strong tower — the refuge of a poor and needy sinner; it is a golden harp — full of melody; it is a precious ointment — fragrant; to know it is eternal life. His kingdom is righteousness, peace, and joy in the Holy Ghost; and when it is come, it will be a manifest reign and glory on earth. His will is my salvation and sanctification; His will is to work in me both to will and to do. The fulfilment of these petitions involved His bitter sufferings and His agony on the cross; for in the death of Jesus the name of God is fully declared, the love of God is revealed and secured. If Jesus had not worn the crown of thorns, if He had not been lifted up to the cross, how could the kingdom ever be established on our sinful and enthralled earth } And how could God's will be realized unless Jesus had first come "to do God's will," even the eternal counsel, which appointed Him to be the Lamb slain for us } How difficult, then, were these petitions for Jesus! how easy are they for us! and yet how sincerely, how ardently He desired them! Will you hesitate to offer the blood-bought petitions?

Has the soul thus mounted into the golden heights, then, centred in God, delighting itself in the Lord, it is anxious about nothing, but with prayer and supplication makes known its wants unto the Father. Jesus had not where to lay His head; He needed food and raiment and shelter, and sometimes a piece of money to pay tribute. And He felt responsible for the dear disciples who had left all and followed Him; so He said to the Father, "Give us this day our daily bread." And did the disciples ever lack while they were with Him? So may and must we pray for our bodily and temporal wants, in the spirit of contentment, of charity, and of faith — bread, our bread, to-day; in the spirit of moderation, and not hasting to be rich; of liberality, and not thinking merely of self; of calmness, without feverish anxiety for the future. Here come in all petitions for health, for work, for direction and prosperity in our daily occupations.

But the Saviour felt the burden of the world's sin. Sinless and pure Himself, He saw iniquity abounding. He saw His own disciples continually trespassing. And what was His desire? On the cross He prayed for His enemies, and all the patience and long-suffering of God are based upon Christ's mediation. The petition of Christ is, that sinners may so know and experience the forgiving love of God as to become themselves forgiving and merciful; that since sin has entered, the healing and restoring grace of salvation may bring pardon and peace to the children of men. And then He thinks of the dangers and temptations and the evil with which His people have to contend as long as they are in the body. He commends them to God's guidance; He asks for deliverance and victory. And thus He returns into the bosom of His Father, to fulness of rest and joy, in the blessed assurance of a perfect answer; for Himself is the Amen. So are we to pray for forgiveness of our daily offences, and immediately vow to the Lord to put on, as the elect of God, bowels of mercy, forgiving and forbearing. We are to pray against temptation, and for deliverance from evil; and we are to conclude with a firm conviction and peaceful assurance of God's answer. As is your Amen, so has been your prayer. Prayer in the name of Christ ends with a calm and joyous Amen; for Jesus Himself is the Amen of God, in whom all promises and gifts of God are sealed.

Learn then to pray with Christ, in harmony with the man Christ Jesus, the great Mediator and Head of the family, and you will not merely pray in His name, you will also *live* in Christ's name. If we pray after this manner we shall possess faith, love, hope; we shall commune with our own hearts, and examine ourselves; ours will be an unworldly and calm spirit; we shall be grave, watchful, solemn, yet rejoicing in hope of the glory of God; gentle and lowly, forgiving and forbearing. Like Jesus! Oh, brethren, is God Father? is Jesus the Lamb? is the Spirit a Dove? and are *we* to be and to remain proud, selfish, hard, easily provoked, and earthly-minded? Oh let us draw nigh to God, and be the children of the Most High!

Be encouraged, and let not your hearts be straitened.

"Lo, the great High Priest ascended,
   Pleads the merit of His blood."

He ever liveth to make intercession for you. Before you approach the throne of grace He has already mentioned your name to the Father; before your feeble voice is lifted up His all-prevailing intercession is heard of God. See the incense of the Lord's intercession and your prayer will rise up with and in His prayer, a sweet savour unto the Father. And doubt not, but believe, that the Lord heareth His Anointed.

"High Priest of the Church Dispensation,
   Lift up, we pray. Thy pierced hand,
And bless Thy ransomed congregation
   In every place, by sea and land.
Before Thy Father's face remember
By name each individual member;
Thy face now on us shine,
Grant us Thy peace divine;
    For we are thine." [5]

How frequently God commands and encourages us to draw nigh to Him! He never blames the importunity and perseverance of prayer. We cannot ask too much, or too often, or too earnestly. How often does He even mourn over Israel's want of prayer and believing supplication? If they only had asked Him, He would soon have vanquished their enemies, He would gladly have enriched them with His gifts. So does God condescend to our language, to assure us that He delights in hearing our prayer. And if He seems not to hear, or to chide, or to refuse, it is only to prepare you for a fuller and more gracious answer. Be not discouraged. Have you asked, and is God silent? Perhaps you are one of the chosen, who are specially near to Him. Remember how he said to Mary, What have I to do with thee? And wait. He will soon show forth His glory and gladden your heart. Remember how He was silent to the Syrophoenician woman, and then refused her, as not belonging to the chosen people, and called her dog, and how after these dark clouds the sun burst forth so brightly. "O woman, great is thy faith," He exclaimed with joyous admiration and omnipotent grace. Remember how He made as if He would go further, and yet was so easily constrained to join with the disciples; how He made Himself known in the breaking of bread. Remember how Paul besought Him thrice, and there was given him far more and better than he asked: "My grace is sufficient for thee; for my strength is made perfect in weakness." Draw nigh to God.

We are encouraged to draw nigh to God by all the saints o{ God, whose history is recorded in Scripture. All the stars that shine in the firmament for ever were once men of like passions as we are, struggling, sinful, suffering believers. What shall we say of Abraham our father? Is he not called the friend of God? Was not his life of faith a life of childlike, reverent, and trustful prayer? How did Jacob become Israel but by wrestling with the angel? Why did the countenance of Moses shine but because he had been on the mount of God? How did he lead Israel through the Red Sea but by faith, because, although his lips were silent, his heart cried unto the Lord? The harp of David still sounds in our ear; and the Holy Ghost has crystallized for us the prayers and praises of the son of Jesse. Some one said that architecture was music frosted. The Psalms are the music of the heart, sometimes plaintive and sad, sometimes joyous and jubilant, sometimes full of anguish and darkness, sometimes tranquil and happy — the music of David's soul preserved by the Spirit, that hearing it we may feel encouraged to draw nigh to God. Daniel was a man greatly beloved, and of great desire. The highest position, in the greatest and most complicated monarchy, did not keep him from daily, frequent supplication. What explains to us the secret of Paul's wisdom, zeal, love, success, and strength in suffering, but his prayer without ceasing, his constant bowing the knees of his heart before God? All the saints of God who are now in glory have only one secret to tell us, only one, "Draw nigh to God, and He will draw nigh to you."

I think of the whole history of Israel. How often they forgot God, the Rock of their salvation. But whenever they cried unto Him, He heard them; He never failed. He never dealt with them according to their sins. He forgot their ingratitude; but He remembered His covenant with Abraham, His tender mercies and compassion. What an illustration of the words of James: "If any man lack wisdom, let him ask of God, who giveth to all simply, and upbraideth not, and it shall be given him." "The giving God, who giveth simply," (i. 5.) He giveth just because He is asked, in all simplicity, and in giving upbraideth not for our past ingratitude and sin.

Dear children, draw nigh to Jesus. Many prayers have been offered up for you by parents and teachers and friends; without your knowing it, you have been often carried before the Lord, that He may bless you. Now that you can understand the words of the Saviour, "Suffer little children to come unto Me," draw nigh to God. Do not wait till you are grown up. To draw nigh to God, it is not necessary for children to become old; it is necessary for the old to become children. Before God we are all little, ignorant, weak; alas! we are all sinful, selfish, and guilty. But just as we are we come, and He forgives us for Jesus' sake, and renews our hearts. When Solomon asked God for a wise and understanding heart, God was pleased, and told him that He *had* given it to him because he asked it. If you really ask God for a new heart, He will give you a new heart. Children, draw nigh to God. Remember —

"Around the throne of God in heaven
    Thousands of children stand;"

and of them it is said —

"On earth they sought the Lord by prayer."

Draw nigh to God, that so you may dread the grave as little as your bed. Draw nigh to God, that you may live a happy and useful life. Children who come to God, are often spared a long time on earth to serve Him. Samuel drew nigh to God when he was a little child: "Speak, Lord; for thy servant heareth;" and he was a prophet and ruler in Israel for ninety years.

"Now that my journey 's but begun,
    My course so little trod,
I'll stay, before I further run,
    And give myself to God."

Young people, draw nigh to God. None ever regretted that in his youth he sought God and found Him. Strange to say, even those who have afterwards forgotten God and become unbelievers think that religion is good, salutary, and necessary for the young; and if they can look back on a childhood and youth of prayer, they are not ashamed of it. Ah! believe it, that now is the time for you to draw nigh to God, to listen to the voice of Wisdom, to bend your wayward and restless heart to the sweet will of God our Saviour, to be built on the Rock of ages, and to take hold of the promises of God, which are yea and Amen in Christ Jesus. Draw nigh to God, that He may give you a heart to love and serve Him, that He may graft you a living branch into the true Vine. No principle will ever make you happy, or give you strength to resist temptation; you need Jesus Himself. You have read the story of Hercules, and the choice between the narrow path of virtue and the broad way of pleasure. This was the best the ancient world knew. They knew nothing of conversion, of a crucified Saviour, who not merely shows the way, but who *is* the way, who by His love makes us love Him, and who Himself is our life and strength. What a blessed thing for you that you know of Jesus, if by Him you draw nigh to God!

You parents, God has placed part of His crown on your heads, and commanded the children to honour and obey you. Go for them and with them to the throne of grace. You who are in the active duties and various trials of life, draw nigh to God. As you grow older, do not become colder, but more fervent. Seek not great things, either for yourselves or your children, and beware of the worldly spirit.

Remember that man's life does not consist in what he has, but in what he is. Serve Jesus and the Church. Oh, let not the best years of your life be years in which you have little communion with God, and in which you do little for Christ! "Lay up for yourselves treasures in heaven." Let not your biography be summed up: "He turned to God in his youth, he then became lukewarm, being engrossed in the cares and the business and the social demands of the world, and a short time before his death he saw his mistake, and felt that one thing was needful. For years his spiritual life was barely sustained by the prayers of friends and the weekly services of the sanctuary. He might have been a pillar in the Church, but he was only a weight." This be far from you. Oh, serve the Lord with gladness, be strong, quit yourselves like men, and abound in the work of the Lord! "Draw nigh to God."

And you, aged pilgrims, honoured and beloved, draw nigh to God; and though it is evening, and the day is far spent, Jesus will make all shadows flee away, and your hearts will burn with love and joy. God renews our youth. Of Moses it is written: "And Moses was an hundred and twenty years old when he died: his eye was not dim, nor his natural force abated." And Caleb, who followed the Lord fully, said to the people of Israel, when he was eighty and five years old: "As yet I am as strong this day as I was in the day that Moses sent me." [6] Spiritually, this is true of all God's aged saints. They that wait on the Lord renew their strength. All the characteristics of youth are theirs — fulness of life, and an abundant and lively hope. The world knows of no source of rejuvenescence; they regard the sunset with melancholy resignation. Youth appears rich in enjoyment, in plans, in hopes, in manifold and full life; old age, on the other hand, poor, colourless, and weak. But it is not so with the aged servants of God. They have been enriched with the treasures of divine knowledge and spiritual experience; their interest in God's kingdom has increased deeper and broader. Although the outward man is perishing, yet the inward man is renewed day by day. They are strong in the Lord; they know Him who is from the beginning; they possess a hope which maketh not ashamed; they feel the nearness of the land of perfect peace.

In conclusion, let us hear the voice of an eminent servant in Christ, who, on his deathbed, thus spoke to his friends: [6] "If I were to return to life, I would, with the help of God and in distrust of myself, give much more time to prayer than I have hitherto done, reckoning much more upon the effect of that than on my own labour; which, however, it is our duty never to neglect, but which has no strength but in as far as it is animated by prayer. I would especially strive to obtain in my prayers that unction, that fervour of the Holy Spirit which is not learned in a day, but is the fruit of a long, and often a painful, apprenticeship. Oh, my friends! you who are full of life — you whose career does not seem to be near its end — lay hold of the opportunity and redeem it; cultivate new habits of prayer. Bring into prayer, with a spirit of fervour, a spirit of order and method that will increase its power, as it increases the power of all human things, and co-operates with the Divine agency itself; that method and arrangement of which Jesus Christ has given us an example in the model He left us — the Lord's prayer."

[1] "What wond'rous grace! Who knows its full extent?
   A creature, dust and ashes, speaks with God —
   Tells all his woes, enumerates his wants,
   Yea, pleads with Deity, and gains relief.
   'Tis prayer, yes, 'tis 'effectual, fervent prayer,'
   Puts dignity on worms, proves life divine,
   Makes demons tremble, breaks the darkest cloud,

And with a princely power prevails with God!
And shall this privilege become a task?
My God, forbid! Pour out thy Spirit's grace.
Draw me by love, and teach me how to pray.
Yea, let Thy holy unction from above
Beget, extend, maintain my intercourse
With Father, Son, and Spirit, Israel's God,
Until petitions are exchanged for praise." — IRONS.

[2] "Lord, what a change within us one short hour
Spent in Thy presence will prevail to make,
What heavy burdens from our bosoms take,
What parched grounds refresh, as with a shower!
We kneel, and all around us seems to lower;
We rise, and all the distant and the near
Stands forth in sunny outline, brave and clear;
We kneel, how weak! we rise, how full of power!
Why, therefore, should we do ourselves this wrong,
Or others, that we are not always strong,
That we are ever overborne with care.
That we should ever weak or heartless be.
Anxious or troubled, when with us is prayer.
And joy, and strength, and courage are with Thee?"

Trench.

[3] Compare context, v. 7, "Resist the devil, and he will flee from you."

[4] Cowper says,

> "Satan trembles when he sees
> The weakest saint upon his knees."

This may seem to contradict our experience. Satan is busy tempting and distracting us when we approach God. And this also belongs to the various hindrances we meet in drawing to the mercy-seat. But when we have overcome these difficulties, when we have really got access to the throne of God, when we are *within,* when we pray in praying, then it is that our enemies cannot reach and harm us. Yet even then let us rejoice with fear and trembling, with humility and watchfulness.

[5] Moravian Hymn.

[6] Joshua xiv. 9.

[7] A. Monod's *Farewell.*

Chapter Four - The Fulfilment of the Promise

"And He will draw nigh to you." — James iv. 8.

And is it so? Does God fulfil His promise? The whole family in heaven and on earth answer, Yes; "I love the Lord, because He hath heard my voice and my supplications."

It is a blessed thing to draw nigh unto God; but it is still more blessed when God draws nigh to us. Even the faintest approach to God, although in darkness and out of the depths, is blessed; it is because God draws, because His grace, unknown as yet, goes before, that we ever draw nigh. The prayer, by which divine love is conquered, is itself inspired by God's Spirit. For this reason the Lord pronounces the poor in spirit blessed, the mourners, and those which hunger and thirst after righteousness. He calls them blessed, because there is an absolute certainty that God will draw nigh to them. The consolation, the feast, all things are ready for them. Nay, strictly speaking, theirs is even now the kingdom of heaven; they think they are only seekers, but they have been found by divine grace, and they will surely find.

All religions say, "Draw nigh to God." The wonderful peculiarity of Christianity (and Jehovahism) is, that it calls on man to draw nigh to God, *because* He has drawn nigh to us. God reveals Himself as a sin-forgiving and heart-renewing God — as love. True worship starts with the assurance of divine favour; at least, with the knowledge that there is full grace in God. False religions always regard this as the object and ultimate point to be gained gradually through man's drawing nigh by prayer, sacrifice, and works. Man tries to ascend, to work his way upwards by steps, winding, broken, endless: God comes down to us with the invitation and gift of perfect love. In Jesus only we have the full and blessed reality and assurance, God will draw nigh to us. Christ is a living Saviour. He gives what He promises. His messengers do not merely exhort; but they testify of a present heaven. They not merely direct to the Physician; but they ask you to test by experience that He can heal and restore. They do not say. Go; but they say. Come. Penetrate, then, into the sanctuary. Rest not satisfied with drawing nigh to God, but obtain the promise.

The golden gates stand open; they are beautiful, but the home to which they lead is more glorious. It is prepared for all who enter. The casket is attractive, and resplendent with the hidden beauty it contains; but what when compared with the pearl of great price which is within? Let Faith only open the casket, and you not merely behold, but possess the precious treasure. The passer-by is arrested by the fragrance of flowers and the song of birds. Bid farewell to the love of sin and the world by looking unto Jesus, and you are within the blood-sprinkled enclosure in the garden of the Lord. Out of the wilderness, you are transplanted into the kingdom of God. "Draw nigh to God, and God will draw nigh to you." You will be within, and no longer outside. Oh, believe it, this is the only thing absolutely certain and attainable on earth — this is the only thing in which we can be perfectly successful! We seek pleasure and earthly happiness, and cannot find and secure it; we seek to be great or good, and cannot attain it. But if we seek Christ, we must and we do find Him; and Christ is all. The only thing we can secure on earth is heaven. If we draw nigh to God, God does draw nigh to us. True, when He comes He takes from us all we have — our righteousness, our peace, our life.

Before we possess the hidden life; we must die with Christ. He crucifies the world to us, and He crucifies us to the world; but He gives us Himself, and Himself is all — more than all; for it is He who makes "all" to be "all." Now the soul that has sighed, "Oh that I knew where to find Him!" says, "Whom have I in heaven but Thee? and there is none upon earth whom I desire beside Thee."

In the Scriptures, written by the inspiration of the God of love and wisdom, there are encouragements and invitations, so simple, affectionate, and comprehensive, that none can remain in doubt as to their meaning; that none can fail to see the willingness of God to receive and bless the returning sinner. They are clear and frequent; human language can afford no terms more lucid, urgent, and tender. Beside these texts, written so legibly and attractively on the door of revelation, there are other declarations of Scripture which are understood and enjoyed only by those who, obedient to the heavenly voice, have entered in by the open gate. There are, so to say, outside texts and inside texts.

"Wisdom standeth in the top of high places, by the way in the places of the paths." Wisdom cries and puts forth her voice; she speaks unto all. "Unto you, O men, I call; and my voice is to the sons of men." To the simple and to fools she speaks of excellent things. Thus God does not speak in secret places, not in heights inaccessible, and depths which we cannot fathom. "The Word is nigh thee." As Jesus said, "I taught daily in the temple." God speaks daily to us, where we must hear His voice. God speaks with such directness and simplicity, addressing the *sensus communis,* and commanding the immediate assent of the inner man. And God speaks to all, excluding none, however foolish or sinful.

Here all is open, universal; but if we listen to this voice of wisdom, we enter, and, no longer among the multitude and crowd of the streets, on the dusty and noisy highway, we shall be in the presence of God, in the school of Christ. The Father will reveal to us the mystery of Christ, and the secret of the Lord shall be with us by the teaching of the Holy Spirit.

"God so loved the world, that He gave His only-begotten Son, that whosoever believeth in Him shall not perish, but have everlasting life." What can be more encouraging and comprehensive than this divine message? Here is indeed a wide, open, golden gate! But if we. enter, we read, "The life of faith in the Son of God, who loved me, and gave Himself for me!' If we did not possess the outside and comprehensive texts, Scripture would be like a house without a door. However firm the foundation, solid the walls, secure the roof; however beautiful and capacious the rooms, the wanderer outside in darkness, loneliness, and danger, seeking shelter and peace, could not enter. But if Scripture did not contain the inside, special, and mysterious texts, it would be like doors that lead to nothing, promises which have no fulfilment, invitations to a feast without the reality of a feast awaiting those who accept them. It would be merely "Come;" but not "All things are ready."

We need not expect to read the inside texts until we are inside. [1] The love of Jesus, what , it is — none but His loved ones know. That which describes the experience of the believer and the dealings of God with him cannot be known, and cannot form the ground of encouragement to an outsider. God speaks to him as one of the world. God loved the world. Believe, and you will be able to say, Christ loved the Church. He loved me. God speaks to him, as "every one that thirsteth," if you come and buy, you will then know there is a water of life, and the sincere milk of the Word and divine love, which is better than wine.

Yet in God's wisdom the outside texts never become superfluous, even to the saints who are by grace within the fold. The first and simplest truths of the gospel become of growing value to our souls as we advance along the narrow road which leadeth unto life. Truths which are at first received authoritatively, on the evidence of Scripture, become commended to us by their own beauty; and that which we received at first, as it were by force of our own necessity, is found in our progress to be the manifestation of the glory of Christ, so that we are able in measure to contemplate it apart from selfishness, and to see it in the light in which God Himself sees it. How often, I had almost said constantly, has a believer to go back to them. How precious is "God so loved the world" to every saint. How welcome the "whosoever" of the most elementary gospel declaration. "If God had not said, 'Blessed are those that hunger,' I know not what could keep weak Christians from sinking in despair. Many times all I can do is to complain that I want Him, and wish to recover Him." [2] How often we need the encouraging word, "As I live, saith the Lord, I have no pleasure in the death of the sinner, but that he should turn and live." See how the apostle Paul at the end of his long life of service and suffering rejoices in the general declaration, "This is a faithful saying, and worthy of all acceptation, that Christ Jesus has come into the world to save sinners." But how beautifully he changes it into an *inside* text by adding, "of whom I am chief." Yet no believer can be satisfied with the general and, so to speak, introductory texts. If we have really believed, entered in, come to the Saviour, we must know something of what He says and gives to those who belong to Him; we must have experienced the truth of His promise. If we have accepted the invitation, we must have tasted the feast. Here success is absolutely necessary. It is not enough to try; but we must actually enter in by the strait gate. Seeking God, as some one said, is right; but it is not salvation. Jesus is the Saviour, and we must come to Him.

Pascal says: "There are three classes of persons — Those who have found God, and serve Him; those who are busy in seeking Him, but have not found Him; and those who, not having found Him, live without seeking Him. The first are rational and happy; the last are foolish and unhappy; the other class are unhappy, but rational." But we know that every one that seeketh shall find. Let us not deceive ourselves. "Draw nigh to God, and He will draw nigh to you." Come to Jesus, and He gives you rest. Believe in Him, and you have eternal life. Our coming has been no reality, if our receiving is no reality. The answer of God, the response of Jesus, must needs follow the prayer of the soul. Nothing can be more precious than the free, open entrance. And why? Because it does lead to the love of God, to the true peace, and to the eternal life.

Nor are the inside texts without blessing to the seeker. He hears that God has a people; that there are hearts renewed by grace, and inhabited by the Spirit; that there is 'a peace which passeth all understanding; comfort in affliction; hope in death; glory in eternity. The very fact that there is an experience which he has not had yet stirs him up to pray, to seek. Thus Jesus described unto His *disciples,* but *in the hearing of all the people,* the beatitudes of the kingdom. There is a hidden life of the soul; there is communion with God; there is an immediate [3] and real contemplation and enjoyment of divine things; there is a manifestation of Jesus to the believers of which the world has no experience. "My sheep hear my voice."

What is this life? It is not mere knowledge. The word knowledge is often used in Scripture in a high and comprehensive sense; and then to know means, not merely to understand intellectually, or to form a mental conception, but to discern and appropriate by an inward experience, to love and to possess. In this sense, to know is eternal life. [4] This knowledge is the gift of the Holy Spirit, this vision is the fulfilment of the promise, "They shall know Me."

But it would be a fatal mistake if any one consoled himself with the fact, that he understood and accepted the doctrines of the gospel. We may possess much knowledge, yea, all knowledge, even of mysteries, and yet be nothing. Knowledge puffeth up. The kingdom of God is not in word, but in power. "If ye know these things, blessed are ye if ye do them."

Doctrine is, as it were, the form and outline, the shape and vessel; the substance is God Himself. Jesus is the Bread of life, and we must feed on Him. It is not enough to see the bread and the cup, and to know that it is the true nourishment; it is not enough to take it, thus recognising that God freely and lovingly offers it to me as I am; I must eat and drink. We must appropriate Christ. To feed on Christ is an act of the will; it is with the heart that man believeth. [5] This is the secret and inner life, as Jesus saith: "Behold, I stand at the door, and knock: if any man hear my voice, and open the door, I will come in to him, and will sup with him, and he with Me."

God Himself draws nigh; and God only can satisfy the heart. The most subtle idolatry and image-worship is when the soul rests in doctrine, however true. When delighted with the profound and comprehensive scheme of Scripture truth, it forgets that this is but the abstraction, the theory, the shadow of great and living realities. How different is the description of a rose in a botanical manual, however correct, from the beauty and fragrance of a real rose as you hold it in your hand! "Draw nigh to God, and *He* will draw nigh to you" — He Himself, although He may use various channels and instruments; it may be Paul, or Cephas, or Apollos; it may be affliction or prosperity; it may be through the voice of Nature or of Providence; it may be through the word or the example of a Christian; yet it is God Himself. But of all instruments and channels the written Word is of the utmost importance; it stands supreme. It is through Scripture, eminently, that God draws nigh to the soul. But let us never mistake the reading of the Scripture for that real drawing nigh of the living God, towards which it is the great help, and of which it is the great witness. Scripture is not the *substitute* for God's drawing nigh to us, it is only the channel; the written Word of the *past* must become the living Word of the *present*.

There never were more learned, skilful, and laborious interpreters of the Scripture than the scribes and Pharisees. They possessed a very minute knowledge of the written Word, and do not let us forget it, in the main it was correct. They knew which were the greatest commandments; they knew where the Messiah was to be born; they taught so that Jesus could say, Do what they tell you. And yet they did not hear the voice of God. When the Word of God incarnate stood before them, and spoke to them, they rejected Him. Oh, how deeply astonished and grieved was Jesus, the single-hearted and loving child of God, when He discovered this strange anomaly! But He Himself gives us the sad solution of this the most tragic fact of history. [6]

They had not the right aim. They did not seek *God* in the Word, and therefore did not find Him;" they sought the honour that comes from man, and therefore could not believe. They loved the present world; and it is only in proportion as we have died unto the world that we can understand and love God's truth. They were anxious to be thought masters and expositors; and even when they tried to find out the practical meaning of Scripture, it was to solemnize and edify others, and not themselves. They prepared dainties for others, while they were starving themselves; they pointed to others the way, and remained only dead and wooden sign-posts. They came to Scripture, as Nicodemus came to Jesus, acknowledging that it was a book come from God, expecting Information and improvement, not knowing that they needed to be born again. [8] They quoted commentaries, and stole the Word one from the other, saying, the burden of the Lord, this is the text and the interpretation; and never prayed, Open Thou mine eyes; and never sought a message from the living God: "Open Thou my lips; and my mouth shall shew forth Thy praise."

Such was Pharisaism. But when God draws nigh, when It pleases Him to reveal His Son in us, then we count the erudition so eagerly acquired at the feet of Gamaliel but dross; we become God's children, Christ's disciples, and the Spirit of God teaches us that wisdom which the world counts foolishness.

God speaks In and through the Word. It Is not that God spake long ago, and that the record of His acts and words. His revelation, was embodied in a perfect manner, and preserved for us in Scripture. This is true. But God gave us the Bible, not to be silent now and let the Bible speak *instead* of Him, and be a *guarantee* for Him, but that He Himself may through His word speak, comfort, and confirm the soul, filling it with His light and love.

Did not David possess and love the five books of Moses? yet did he not continually pray, "Be not silent unto me"? Because we have Scripture, we say, "I will hear what God the Lord will say." Does not the author of the 119th Psalm express it in more than a hundred ways? "Thou hast given me Thy blessed word; speak to me — teach, guide, enlighten me. From Thee direct, from Thee, living and loving One, I seek all through Thy word — not from the ancients or tradition, not from the seniors or authority."

It is God's word, and therefore all is *profitable* to us at present. Every incident, every character, every promise, every command, is a present and living reality to us. Not for the preacher, not for the theologian, not for the literary man, not for the man of taste, not for the man of principle, but for the *man of God*, is Scripture inspired. It is to make us the children of the Most High, to make us Christ-like, to conform us to the image of His Son, to furnish us throughly unto every good work; so that after the discipline of this earthly life we may be made manifest in glory,

God draws nigh in the Word. Do we know what it is to read the Bible in the original? It does not mean in Hebrew or Greek. God speaks neither Hebrew nor Greek. This is the original language of Scripture — the love of God to the soul: "I have loved thee with an everlasting love: therefore with loving-kindness have I drawn thee." And all God's vocabulary is summed up in Jesus — Alpha and Omega, He is *the Word*. When God takes the written Word back from the paper into His own mouth, then we read the original; then it is again God breathed, and the word which Cometh out of His mouth shall not return void.

None but the Lord our God can teach us to profit. People advise us how to read the Bible. They suggest, probably from their own experience, various methods and plans how to study the Bible. External knowledge of Scripture is very valuable, but let us not rest in it. Method is useful, but let us not be taken up with it. Rather let us look to our motive in reading Scripture. We do not want knowledge to shine before men, but to be humble before God. Let us consult the living commentaries brought before us in God's providence — our work, our friends, our lives. And as prayer is only the culminating point of our drawing nigh to God, so the reading of Scripture is only the culminating point of God's drawing nigh to us; for the living God connects His providence, our daily life, work, and suffering, with His word. If, as Jesus says, he that docs the will of God shall know of His doctrine, then we may be assured that the diligent, conscientious, and prayerful performance of our daily duties will be made the preparation for receiving greater and deeper blessings in the reading of God's word. It is not time and leisure we want. If we are in the Spirit, if we draw nigh to God, God can draw nigh unto us in one little text, in the remembrance of one Bible narrative or promise, in the remembrance of one single feature of the Lord's countenance and character, and fill our souls with marrow and fat.

As we read of the Lord Jesus, that He fed the multitude of thousands with five loaves and two fishes, and all were satisfied, and there remained seven baskets of fragments, so God can make a few Scripture verses, or a single promise, supply abundantly all our need, be it of guidance in perplexing" circumstances, or of strength under exhausting difficulties, or of consolation in heart-sorrow. And not merely supply our need, but so fill us with divine light and grace, that with this single Word we shall go and enrich and comfort others, so that nothing of God's marvellous bounty is lost.

Scripture itself teaches us how to use Scripture. It is in Scripture that we find the deepest and most far-reaching protests against a superstitious and mechanical, against a merely intellectual and sentimental, reading of the Bible.

In the Psalms of David especially, God has given to us a perfect picture of the spiritual use of Scripture. [9]

Take the first psalm. It is most solemn and awful. It describes the broad road and the narrow way; the wheat and the chaff; the judgment which shall separate with unerring and inexorable severity, gathering the precious into the garner, and burning the chaff with unquenchable fire. Who is the godly man? He is characterized not by fear and terror, but by an indwelling, bright, and peaceful joy. That which really separates him from the wicked, is the secret treasure he has found in God's love. His *delight* is in the law of the Lord. He meditates on it day and night. Even by night; for our spiritual life is deeper than our consciousness. Thus God draws nigh unto him, and sustains and guides him in all his ways. Thus, while no human eye sees the vitalizing and refreshing element in which his soul is rooted, every one beholds his strength, his good works, his peaceful and rhythmical life; "like a tree planted by the rivers of water, that bringeth forth his fruit in his season; his leaf also shall not wither; and whatsoever he doeth shall prosper."

Look again at the nineteenth Psalm. David hears the voice of the living God in the world or nature around him, in the Scripture, and in the heart within. He rejoices in God, who is not silent to him. Always and everywhere he hears the voice, he sees the glory, he sees the grace. The heavens declare it to him, and the sun, emblem of the light and love of God, of the Bridegroom of the soul, of the free gospel, [10] preaches to him glad tidings. He can understand the voice of Nature, because Scripture taught him *God*. The word of God, enlightening and renewing, rejoicing the heart, and guiding the walk, has become more precious to him than gold, sweeter than honeycomb. This would be superstition and idolatry, as well as self-deception, were it not that *God* reveals and bestows Himself in the Word. This voice speaks to *him* personally; and therefore he looks *within,* and in humility he prays, "Who can understand his errors? cleanse thou me from secret faults." And in all this he has been speaking both before and to God. "Let the words of my mouth, and the meditation of my heart, be acceptable in Thy sight, O Lord, my strength and my redeemer."

Look at the 119th Psalm, the golden A B C of the Jews. This, as every one knows, is the *longest* psalm; but let us see that it is also a *great* psalm. It extols the excellency of the word of God; and in doing so, describes the nature, power, and blessing of Scripture in a most comprehensive manner. God, man, and Scripture, human life in all its aspects, and the divine Word — these are the topics of the psalm. He begins (Aleph) by stating the ideal of the godly life, to be undefiled in the way, seeking God with the whole heart, keeping God's statutes, having respect unto all His commandments — the man of God throughly furnished unto every good work, and that by the Word, And then (Beth), starting with youth, its ignorance, sinfulness, and temptations, he goes through all human experiences, and shows how God's word sanctifies and comforts, helps and directs us. The temptations of sin, the snares of the world, the reproach of the ungodly, the contempt of the wicked for God's truth, the opposition of the proud and mighty, the false and Pharisaic spirit of the formalists, the afflictions and trials which come from without, the soul's distress and languor, cleaving unto dust, the enlargement of the heart unto willing obedience, the inward calmness and peace of the trustful saint, the joy and jubilant thanksgiving of the soul — all is described here in simplest language of experience. Here is *orbis pictus*. The whole world, outer and inward — and everywhere *God speaking through the Word* — guiding, quieting, sustaining, bringing light and strength and joy. This wonderful psalm is given (and we ought to read it frequently) to make us know what a life-treasure we have in the word of God.

Behold a witness nobler still — the man Christ Jesus. When I think of Him, I wonder how priestly mediation, ecclesiastical authority, human genius and learning, have ever ventured to lord it over God's heritage! "Where is the wise? where is the scribe? where is the disputer of this world?" Christ is our Master and Teacher, the Holy Ghost our Light, and all Christians have the unction from above. Jesus came in humility. He was poor. He was brought up in despised Nazareth. He was called a carpenter. He had no wealth. We easily admit all this, and more or less remember it. But notice, He had no learning. His was no scholastic erudition. He possessed no exegetical lore, and the theologians said of Him, "How does this man know exegesis, having never studied?" Yes; but He was *the man Christ Jesus,* the man of God. He understood the Scriptures, because He drew nigh to God, and God drew nigh to Him. His heart was pure; love to God and man filled His soul. His aim was the Father's glory; His daily meat was to do the will of Him that sent Him. From his childhood he *knew* the Scriptures. Prayer and obedience, humility and love, were his commentaries. He learned in the carpenter's shop of Nazareth, by the daily and hourly guidance of His heavenly Father. His heart was calm and lowly, and the whole light of Scripture was reflected in it. He had the word of God abiding in Him. Jesus teaches us to pray, to draw nigh to God; Jesus teaches us to read the Scriptures, so that God draws nigh to us. When Jesus quotes the Scriptures, it is not merely a quotation of the intellect and of memory, but it is out of His own heart and experience; it is out of His own treasury; it has become His very life-blood, and therefore it is life and light, it is power and authority.

Let us learn of Jesus; let us be like Him; for in order to be like the natural (psychical) man, to whom the Word always remains something external, we need not be regenerated. Our new birth is the commencement of the Christ-life. God hath sent the Spirit of His Son into our hearts. We hear the Father's voice; we pray in Christ's name.

When thus we read Scripture, we feel as if praying; as in the Psalms and Prophets there is constant dialogue, the soul immediately converting the divine message into the response of faith and longing. And when we pray we often feel the Scripture-word brought nigh to our heart, nay, brought Into us, so that we utter it with full consent and central soul-illumination. And thus do we learn to go forth into our life-path, praying without ceasing, and always listening to the heavenly voice.

[1] Many ask questions about election and other doctrines, which do not yet come within their horizon, and therefore cannot be explained to them (to a certain extent, true of us all). The ninth chapter of Paul's epistle to the Romans, as Luther said, *is* the ninth. Learn first the eight chapters which precede it —

   "Soll ich dir die gegend zeigen,
     Musst du erst das Dach besteigen." — Göethe.
   (You cannot see the view unless you ascend the height.)
[2] Bishop Hall.
[3] Immediate. Doctrines having been grasped by the intellect, and received in the heart, we can enter *directly* into communion with God.
[4] John xvii. 3.
[5] When divine truth is presented, the question is not merely, Do I see it? but, Do I will it?
[6] The gospel of John (specially chapters v. and viii.) throws much light on this point. The Lord tells the Jews they have not the word of God abiding *in* them, though they possessed and valued the Scriptures.
[7] "Men are apt to seek everything in the Bible, except God. The man of learning goes to it with his erudition, sees and hears nothing but what gives scope to his art; the inquisitive goes to it with his curiosity, prying into things which the Father hath reserved in His power. Others again seek it in relief from burdensome feelings, and only wish to rejoice in its light for a short season." — Beck.
[8] Francke.
[9] Like the play within the play in *Hamlet,* we see here in the Bible how a godly man reads the Bible.
[10] Rom. x. 18.

Chapter Five - The Experienced Reality of Revelation

"Draw nigh to God, and He will draw nigh to you." - James iv. 8.

Unbelief appears strange to all who know God, because they love Him; to the children of the new covenant, who need no longer that any human authority or instruction should say unto them, "Know the Lord." God has manifested Himself unto them in forgiving their iniquity, and remembering their transgressions no more. Unbelief cannot pray to the living God, and hear the voice of the eternal and ever-speaking Word, the wisdom of God, the Divine Lover of the sons of men. That which is to us the greatest reality, appears a vague and doubtful abstraction to unbelief; it regards as obscure what is to us light, manifesting itself, and making all things manifest; it deems inaccessible and far off what is constantly around us, nay, lives within us — a well of water springing up into eternal life.

And again, this very certainty which we possess, which we in our Christian language call faith, is unintelligible to the merely psychical man. He may sometimes express envy of our happiness, and say he wishes he also could believe; but he thinks that our certainty is either the unreasoning and somewhat infantine rest in an outward authority, or that it is a sentiment of the heart which gives us peace and joy, but which has no foundation in reality. He does not know that faith is the gift of God, a light kindled by the Spirit, who reveals unto us *"the things freely given to us of God."* [1] He does not know that God has spoken to us, and that faith cometh by hearing this voice. He is therefore not able to understand how the Spiritual man, who by reason of a new birth sees the kingdom of God, knoweth of a certainty all things, and how all the objections, doubts, and difficulties of the learned do not touch him or even disturb his mind. And this is his knowledge, there is the living God; prayer and the word of God are experienced realities; he has tested the Word, "Draw nigh to God, and He will draw nigh to you."

Into this simple question all must finally resolve itself: Is there the living God? If we believe that God lives, then we shall experience, God hath spoken, and we shall also experience that He is the hearer of prayer. If we do not know the living God, all our acknowledgment of Scripture is superficial, and we have not yet heard that voice which begets faith, nor do we know the blessedness of prayer, of that constant life in God's presence, and conscious dependence on Him.

God manifests Himself to the simple, the ignorant — unto babes; and His self-manifestation must be of such a nature, that no human authority is needed to attest it, or human learning to defend it. Is the faith of a simple Christian shaken because difficulties of science or metaphysics, of history or chronology, are brought forward — is his faith suspended until they are answered? Has there been a single century in which unbelief had not many difficulties, and some very subtle and specious, to urge against the truth? Has the Church, though able to answer all arguments, been able to alter the doubting heart and the God-estranged mind, which ever invents new difficulties, and ever changes its method and weapons of attack? But all this time has not the Church believed without hesitation and faltering, because the true Light now shineth, and the Spirit beareth witness, because the Spirit is truth.

Christians know God, and Jesus the heavenly Friend! The Holy Spirit has revealed unto us the Father and the Son. We know the Word also, in which He has made us to hope, and least of all can the vain philosophy of the world move us; for this very unbelief is foretold. Could human wisdom receive and defend the truth, the Holy Ghost would not be needed; but the simplest and most uncultured may, by the grace of God, have perfect assurance, light, the knowledge, "God hath spoken to me."

I am well aware that men are always wishing to find some other foundation than that which is laid. They wish something over and beyond the word of God wherein to trust. They wish us to prove that Scripture is the word of God. It is as if you asked any one to prove the brightness of the sun, or the loudness of thunder, or the sweetness of honey. The word of God proves itself divine. But again it is objected: Because it has proved itself thus to you, it may not prove itself to me. We answer: If any man thirst, let him come and taste that the Lord is gracious. He who speaks to you in the Word is no stranger; it is the Lord who made you. Your mind, your heart, your will, your whole inner man, have been created for God and His word, as much as your eye for light, and your ear for sound. Faith is as natural to your soul as breathing to your lungs.

Man in Paradise heard God's voice, and believed. Doubt was the suggestion of Satan. It is a foreign growth, a poison instilled from without. The enemy hath sown this. "Hath God said?" or *skepsis,* or criticism of the divine Word, is not the development of something originally human, but the sophism of the old serpent. Truly, it is not merely the first impression from a mother's loving teaching that makes it difficult for men to give up faith in God, in His word, in prayer. There is the great and glorious fact, that God has indeed spoken; that He who made the heart has had *first* entrance to it; that He has spoken *first;* that, as in a palimpsest, deep, deep below all the writing of doubt and unbelief is the writing of God, and shall remain there, either in an eternity of blessedness or anguish.

When believers, who walk with God, testify of their inward experience of the reality of divine revelation, it may seem at first as if they were deficient in the wisdom of love, which adapts itself to the position and capacity of the hearer. But both Scripture and experience teach us that such is the best and most loving method. We are bound to remove difficulties and to answer objections. It is profitable also to point out those peculiarities and excellencies in the Scriptures, which distinguish them as unique in kind, and unparalleled in the literature of the world. It is right to bring forward the great and unanswerable evidence of prophecy, which is miracle stereotyped for the reading of all generations. It is instructive and stimulating to review the wonderful effects produced through this book in every age of the world's history, among all nations, and on every variety of mankind — ignorant and learned, high and low, young and old. The outward bulwarks and fortresses, defending the citadel of Scripture, are strong and impregnable; the inward beauty and excellence, of unequalled magnitude and attractiveness. And yet, to use the words of one of the Confessions of the Reformation, [2] when the authority of the Scriptures was held in so scriptural a way, as connected with the supreme authority, power, and light of the Holy Ghost: "We may be moved and induced by the testimony of the Church to an high and reverend esteem of the holy Scripture, and the heavenliness of the matter, the efficacy of the doctrine, the majesty of the style, the consent of all the parts, the scope of the whole (which is to give all glory to God), the full discovery it makes of the only way of man's salvation, the many other incomparable excellencies, and the entire perfection thereof, are arguments whereby it doth abundantly evidence itself to be the word of God; yet, notwithstanding, our full persuasion and assurance of the infallible truth and divine authority thereof is from the inward work of the Holy Spirit, bearing witness by and with the Word in our hearts."

He who accepts the Scriptures on external evidence, including even the sublimity of the doctrine it contains, without experiencing in his heart that God is in the present speaking to him in this written Word, still stands without, and has not yet received the testimony of the Spirit. Scripture is still an external authority to him, because as yet the word of God as such has not been received, and does not abide in his heart. [3] Our great object Is to testify to such that God lives; that He who spake of old by the prophets, and at last in His Son, who gave a record of His revelation in the Scriptures, now reveals Himself by the Word to the soul, when the Spirit manifests Christ to our hearts. We are sent to testify of Christ according to the Scripture; not to defend the Scripture, which points to Christ.

Hence that which is our great message is not in the region of human argument and ratiocination, criticism, and evidence, although connected with it; it announces an experience, a new life; it is received by a new birth; it is accompanied by the heavenly power and demonstration of the Holy Ghost. [4]

God lives: this is the testimony of the Church. He lives, and He is Love. Hence we believe in miracle, God interfering in redemptive mercy; in prophecy, God interfering in redeeming wisdom. [5] We believe that God speaks to us, and gives unto us deliverance from sin and evil, and the assurance of His favour; nay, we experience that we live before, wath, and in Him. We believe that what corresponds to the longings and desires of our minds and hearts is not anything abstract and impersonal, but the living God Himself. "He that formed the eye," we say with the psalmist, "shall He not see?" Not, Is He not *light?* but. Is He not the Seeing One? "He that planted the ear, shall He not hear?" What corresponds to the eye, or the light-receptive, light-desiring element in man, is another Eye, full of light, all-seeing. What alone responds to the love of man is God, who is Love. What alone can renew and heal man's will is another Will, even God, who worketh all things of His good pleasure. Thus from the very outset we are drawn to the solemn and most blessed conclusion, that God, infinite above us, is to be known and experienced by love, by His dwelling within us. [6]

Why should it be deemed strange that there is communion between God and man, when the deepest and simplest knowledge we have of God is, "God is love" (and love is never silent); when the truest conception we can form of man is, that He is created in the image of God? What are all laws compared with this fundamental law — nay, so to speak, this source and origin of all law — "God is love"? Or, what is there in man, who alone of all earthly creatures lifts up his eye to heaven, that renders it impossible or improbable that God should speak to him and hear his voice? And where else but in this communion can the human heart find rest? Are we not constantly seeking in the created, and seeking in vain, that Thou, who can understand and satisfy the heart, who can be loved supremely, and whose love can be an ever-increasing joy and blessedness to us, to us, who have to confess —

"Not e'en the dearest heart, and next our own,
Knows half the reason why we smile or sigh"?

Is there no authority and attractive power in the only Voice that says, "Give Me, my son, thy heart." "Thou shalt love the Lord thy God"? [7]

But the question arises. Is such a communion possible? Can fallen and exiled man rise to this height? Can the holy and righteous God thus descend to sinful and guilty man?

How bright is the light which emanates from the Lord Jesus Christ! In Him we behold God manifest in the flesh; in Him we see also man according to the divine idea. The very fact of the Incarnation announces to us the great purpose of God, that we are to be partakers of the divine nature— that a real and eternal communion is to be established between God and man. Is not Jesus in His own person the full realization of the word, "Draw nigh to God, and He will draw nigh to you"?

Is not His whole life a life of communion with God, so that He always is, speaks, and works in the Father, and the Father in Him? And does not this, His inexistence in the Father, prepare us for the mystery which He revealed "plainly" and without parable on that memorable evening, that He came from the Father, and again was going to the Father, and to the glory which He had with Him before the foundation of the world? When we thus behold the man Christ Jesus, and believe that He is the Son of God, does not the hope arise in our hearts, that He came, not to abide alone, not merely to manifest the Father and the divine eternal life, wrought into humanity, but to *communicate* this life unto us, so that we also, through and in Him, should have communion with God? How gladly do we then receive the mystery of His death and resurrection, that by the sacrifice of Himself Jesus has taken away all that separated us from God, and has Himself become the new and living way of access unto the Father; that by His resurrection He became the First-born among many brethren, and that, as the quickening Spirit, He is now our life.

Here is the point from which all revelation is seen as possible and real. It was only after the disciples understood the mystery of Christ's death and resurrection, that they "understood the Scriptures." They had always believed the Scriptures to be the "oracles of God," and regarded them with profound veneration as the very word of the Most High. They had gathered around Jesus, drawn by the sweet and irresistible magnet of His light and love, and an inward conviction made them exclaim joyfully, "We have found the Messiah — Him of whom Moses in the law, and the prophets, did write!" And yet, as the evangelist John testifies, they did not know the Scripture, even when the words and facts, which they heard and saw, were the clearest and fullest comment on the written record. "Jesus spake of the temple of His body....When therefore He was risen from the dead. His disciples remembered that He had said this unto them; and *they believed the Scripture,* and the Word which Jesus had said." [8]

The same misconception, which fancies a collocation of Messianic passages, and their fulfilment in the New Testament, is all that is needed to convince a modern Jew of the truth of Christianity, prevents a realization of the manner in which the apostles believed. The Messianic passages are indeed numerous, forcible, and, viewed in their connection, they form the grand foundation of apostolic doctrine. But, excepting acquaintance with their general tenor, and the expectation of the Messiah, we may say it was Jesus who led the disciples to the Messianic passages, and not the observed fulfilment of the predictions which brought the disciples to the Lord,

It is the risen Saviour who explains to us the mystery, "through suffering unto glory." This is the key, and the only one, which opens to us the Scriptures. Jesus is the true David, who possesses the key. And while He thus speaks, our hearts burn within us; and it is this glowing heart which receives the indelible impression: Jesus is the Christ of Scripture, and Scripture is the word of God. As truly as Jesus is the Word, the Son of God, the Saviour of sinners, the Source of resurrection-life, so true is it that the Scripture is the divinely-given record, testifying of Him.

"Thus it is written, and thus it behoved Christ to suffer, and to rise from the dead the third day." This is the strong and indissoluble, the tender and thrilling bond, which connects our deepest experience of the revelation and love of God in Christ Jesus, with the inspired Scriptures, Our communion with Jesus introduces us into the full acceptance of the divine record. And as Jesus, in whose name we pray, and who is the fulfilment of our petitions, prayed Himself, and thus is the true Mediator, so Jesus, sum and substance, centre and glory, of the written Word, lived Himself in the constant faith, meditation, and comfort of the Scriptures, and thus leads all His disciples to be followers of Him, knowing the Scriptures and the power of God. [9]

Now Scripture is seen in its beauty, and we feel at *home* in this vast and magnificent temple. From the height of God's eternal counsel, and out of the depth of God's infinite love, Scripture beholds all things, comprehends all ages, and is sufficient for the guidance and perfecting of souls in all generations.

But while we thus stand in awe, beholding the grandeur and infinite depth of the Scripture as one organic spirit-built temple, and the beauty, perfection, and exquisite skill which characterize the most minute portion of this structure, we feel at home and as in a peaceful and fragrant garden. We see Jesus, the Centre, and though many things are obscure, and all things of unfathomable depth, yet all is full of light and peace.

And this also betokens the divine origin of Scripture, that while it forms one organism, every portion of it is complete, is spirit and life. All ages of the Church cannot exhaust its fulness, and yet Timothy knows it from a little child, and is made wise unto salvation. To take comprehensive views is granted unto us at times, but one single verse or psalm, one name of God or promise, brings unto us, as it were, the power and consolation of the whole. Nothing made of man possesses this wonderful peculiarity of the Spirit's work.

There is no book which so reveals to us our inmost self — sin in its depth of guilt and misery — and which at the same time testifies of the love of God, redeeming, healing, and restoring. Nowhere but here do we see the depth of the fall, and the height of glory to which God in His omnipotent grace raises redeemed man. The grandeur of the remedy both unfolds the depth of our misery, and comforts us in our sorrow. Men have often pointed out the sinfulness and wretchedness of man, and they either degrade him, forgetting his high nature and destiny, or leave him in despondency. Where else but in this divine Word do we learn the dignity and elevation of humility before God; so that, lying at the footstool of divine mercy, the contrite and broken heart does not feel degraded, but exalted? Where but here do we see man raised to communion with the Most High — yea, to union with the incarnate Son of God — -and yet retain the spirit of lowliness, of self-condemnation, of utter dependence on divine grace? It is this combination of the full revelation of our sin, disease, and misery, and of the abundant grace of God, which produces in us, in our inmost soul, the *assured conviction of the divine authority of Scripture,* of God's own voice speaking to us in this inspired Word.

No other book is such a mirror both of man and of God. Here we see our own countenance, and we are humbled; here we see the countenance of God, and we are comforted. Here we behold the human heart, with its unbelief, its selfish and carnal thoughts, its tendency to hypocrisy, to seek rest in mere shadows. In reading Scripture, we feel in the presence of Him unto whose eyes all things are naked and open. The Word is like a sharp sword; all that is confused and mixed in our thoughts and hearts is severed, the heavenly separated from the earthly, and the thoughts and intents of the heart discerned. When in this book we read the experiences of God's people, the patriarchs, the wanderings of Israel in the wilderness, the life of David, we feel that we are reading our own history. As Ulysses wept when he heard his own sorrows recited by the minstrel at the court of king Alkinoos, so, as we read in Scripture of the sins, failures, hopes, and fears of God's children, we see our own hearts and lives. When the inner life of God's saints is unveiled to us, as in the Psalms, the Book of Job, the Lamentations of Jeremiah, and indeed throughout Scripture, so that, as Luther says, "we see into the very hearts of these men, and not merely behold paradise and heaven itself there, but also death, and even hell," we possess in these apparently subjective and purely human delineations the teaching of the Holy Ghost, who presents to us truthfully and perfectly the conflict in human souls between God's grace and their sin and weakness, and provides us with a guidebook in which all possible difficulties and errors are noticed, and the true remedies and correctives indicated. Hence no Scripture is purely human and temporary; all Scripture is divine and eternal. It possesses vitality, fulfilling itself continually, and containing throughout the revelation of God's character and of God's salvation. All that Scripture asserts of itself we experience to be true. The Word sifts and divides what no human analysis could separate. It purifies and intensifies the conscience; it exerts a cleansing and vivifying power on our heart and walk. It is like a seed, and we experience that it grows; it does not remain dead and dormant in the memory or understanding; it does not remain a picture, unsubstantial in the imagination, but it manifests vitality, and mingles with all our thoughts, feelings, and actions. It remains ever new, and ever indispensable. The Spirit of God brings it into remembrance, and applies it with power and consoling efficacy. It can still the stormy waves, and bring peace; it can dissipate densest darkness, and we walk in the light, and do not stumble. It is a book for life, for human suffering, work, and trial. It must be lived, and not merely read. It leaves nothing alone; it passes over no phase of experience. It takes cognizance of our very seasons of apathy and of sleep; it brings before us our worst and most hidden thoughts, doubts, and regrets, down to despair; it throws light on everything, and brings salutary medicines for every disease. And thus it becomes to us an engrafted, implanted Word, inseparably connected with the Father, with the living Saviour, and with the indwelling Spirit. God reveals Himself continually to us in the Word — God in Christ and by the Holy Ghost,

The Scripture reaches the highest idea of God's holiness and justice, and of God's tenderness and mercy. It is merciful in its severity; it is holy in its love. Hence the rebukes of Scripture may give pain, and produce godly sorrow; but they do not irritate, embitter, and harden. The consolations of Scripture calm, but they do not weaken and effeminate. The bitter arrows of reproof are sent by the loving hand of the Father; the words of warning are uttered by the voice of yearning compassion, they come from the home of everlasting truth and peace. It is God who speaks, and the love revealed is holy; the righteousness and justice declared, full of truth and mercy.

The Scripture testifies of things unseen, and brings us into contact with heavenly realities. "God being invisible, and the centre and soul of that which is invisible, the difficulty we find in fixing our thoughts upon what is not seen, arises from our being by nature at a distance from God. What characterizes the word of God is, that its life and action are centred in the things not seen; and this fact alone, for a man who reflects, is sufficient to prove its inspiration. It is not given to man, who by his fallen nature became a slave to things that are seen, to rise above them; that is to say, to shake off self sufficiently to rise up to the unseen, and speak from the midst of the invisible world as the word of God does; as not only Jesus Christ the Son of man does, who is in heaven and speaks from heaven, but as do all those agents who are commissioned to transmit to us the word of God, which, being full of Jesus Christ, speaks from heaven, even though upon the earth, by that miracle of the grace of God which we call inspiration, and which constitutes the authority of His word." [10]

The Bible is the divinely-given guide-book; for no other would so constantly point away from itself to the unseen, spiritual, loving Guide; no other would warn us against making it a substitute for the teaching of the Spirit, for the presence of Jesus, for the ever-renewed manifestation of God,

Thus do we experience the reality of the Scripture revelation, unfolding to us, in connection with all God's dealings in Providence, His truth, and comforting us with everlasting consolations. As we advance step by step, God appears greater and more glorious; as we receive out of the fulness of divine wisdom, we feel more that the well is deep, nay, inexhaustible; for we are brought here into contact, not with the powers of man, stretched to the utmost, and giving us their highest conceptions of divine things, but with the Holy Ghost, who searcheth the deep things of God, and revealeth to us, as we can bear it, and as it pleases Him, out of the ocean of divine wisdom.

Here also we feel our profound union with all God-taught Christians, in that very conviction and knowledge of spiritual realities which man cannot give to man — in that community of light and life which in Christ Jesus, the crucified Redeemer, the Father of spirits giveth of His abundant mercy through the Holy Ghost.

[1] I Cor. ii. 12.
[2] The Reformers' teaching on the authority of Scripture was singularly lucid and spiritual. It was the teaching of men who had experienced the reality of divine revelation. Hence, while they opposed the pseudo-mysticism of those who exalted the inward revelation over the letter of Scripture, they always laid great stress on the teaching and power of the Holy Ghost, without whom Scripture is as a sun-dial without the sun.

[3] A very interesting illustration of these remarks will be found in Dr. D. Brown's *Life of the Rev. Dr. Duncan,* page 157, when Dr. Malan said to him, "You have the word of God in your mouth," it passed through me like electricity, that *God meant man to know His mind. Cf.* page 175, &c., where also the same view I have endeavoured to unfold is elucidated by references to John Owen, Halyburton, and Olshausen. In modern times much stress has been laid on the internal evidences, or the self-evidencing light and power of Scripture. This is very valuable, but there may still be in this the rationalistic leaven of the old evidence school. The *internal* evidences are also of no use without the enlightening influence and power of the *Holy Ghost.*

[4] I Cor. ii.

[5] Miracle is not the evidence of what we believe, rather is it the very thing which we believe. It is a constitutive element of our creed, that God Himself, in His omnipotent love, interferes to redeem us from evil, and to renew us after His image. It is not evidence that is wanted to verify the miracle; the very men who saw Lazarus rise from the grave believed not. The organ is wanted to recognise the interference of the living God in saving love. Jesus, after His resurrection, appeared only to His chosen disciples; and they, as *witnesses,* not *defenders* of His resurrection, preached Him according to the Scripture — with the Holy Ghost sent down from heaven.

[6] Jesus speaks of the *eye* as the light of the body — the eye, seeing in God. Man is created for God, to live, move, and be in Him.

[7] "'Love thy God, and love Him only,
   And thy breast will ne'er be lonely.
   In that one great Spirit meet
   All things mighty, grave, and sweet.
      Vainly strives the soul to mingle
   With a being of our kind;
   Vainly hearts with hearts are twined,
      For the deepest still is single.
   An impalpable resistance
   Holds like natures at a distance.
   Mortal! love that Holy One,
   Or dwell for aye alone."   Aubrey de Vere.

[8] John ii. 21-23.

[9] Compare my *Christ and the Scripture,* chap. ii.

[10] A. Monod.

Chapter Six - The Experienced Reality of Prayer

"Draw nigh to God, and He will draw nigh to you." - James iv. 8.

It is a fact worthy of earnest consideration, that Scripture never attempts to remove the doubts and difficulties which human reasoning advances against the efficacy of prayer. The argument which has been brought forward against prayer, in the strict sense of the word — that is, not adoration and contemplation, but petitions offered to God and answered by Him, either from God's omniscience or immutability, or spontaneous and perfect goodness — has so far been anticipated by Scripture, that the facts on which these reasonings seem founded are stated in the word of God with greater clearness, fulness, and uncompromising definiteness, than in any other writings. Where do we meet with such lucid and forcible statements as in Scripture, teaching us that God is omniscient, that He seeth the end from the beginning, and that the inmost thoughts and desires are known to Him, even in their most secret origin, and before we ourselves become conscious of them? [1] How emphatic is the Scripture assertion of God's sovereignty, comprehending all things, and unchangeably foreordaining whatsoever comes to pass in time! "The counsel of the Lord standeth for ever, the thoughts of His heart to all generations." [2] "He worketh all things after the counsel of His own will." [3] How numerous and consoling are the Scripture assurances, that God delights in giving and in showing mercy, and that He is ever bountiful, and that He blesses above all that we can ask or think!

If reason therefore says, in various forms, 'Prayer is unnecessary, because God knows all things, and is full of goodness to bless and to help,' or 'Prayer is of no avail, because there is no room for its action, as all things are ordered and under the reign of fixed and all-wise law,' the difference between reasoning and Scripture is mostly, though not altogether, in the *inferences* deduced from premises, the knowledge of which, in so far as they are accurate, was originally derived from the divine revelation itself.

The Scripture method of dealing with these erroneous inferences is simply to ignore them. As Scripture always pre-supposes faith in the existence of God, so it does not prove the reality and efficacy of prayer, but continually takes belief in it for granted, asserting and illustrating it in every variety of form.

God hears prayer. This simplest view of prayer is taken throughout Scripture. It dwells not on the reflex influence of prayer on our heart and life, although it abundantly shows the connection between prayer as an act, and prayer as a state. It rather fixes with great definiteness the objective or real purpose of prayer, to obtain blessings, gifts, deliverances, from God. "Ask, and it shall be *given* you," [4] Jesus says to us. "Ask what I shall *give* thee," [5] Jehovah said to Solomon. "Call upon Me in the day of trouble, and I will *deliver* thee." [6] "If any man lack wisdom, let him ask...and it shall be *given* him." [7]

Besides commandments so simple and definite in their objective character, we have the clearest statements of *fact* that God answered prayer. The passages stating that God heard prayer are too numerous to quote. In the 107th Psalm the need and misery of man is described under four images, and in each the history is the same: man, brought low, cries to God in his helplessness, and God delivers him. "They cried unto the Lord, and He delivered them out of their distresses." (*vv.* 6, 13, 19, 28.)

All the great manifestations of divine power and grace are connected in Scripture with prayer. Even when prayer is not mentioned in the narrative itself, it is sometimes brought before us in some subsequent portion of Scripture, to remind us of the uniform dealings of God, connecting His grace and power with believing prayer. Thus the prophet Elijah appeared before Ahab with the declaration, "As the Lord God of Israel liveth, there shall not be dew nor rain these years, but according to my word." In the epistle of James we are told that this announcement of faith was the result of fervent prayer. Perhaps the most striking illustration, or rather unveiling, of the power of prayer is in the memorable passages of the prophecy of Daniel: "And whiles I was speaking, and praying, and confessing my sin and the sin of my people Israel, and presenting my supplication before the Lord my God for the holy mountain of my God; yea, whiles I was speaking in prayer, even the man Gabriel, whom I had seen in the vision at the beginning, being caused to fly swiftly, touched me about the time of the evening oblation. And he informed me, and talked with me, and said, O Daniel, I am now come forth to give thee skill and understanding. At the beginning of thy supplications the commandment came forth, and I am come to shew thee; for thou art greatly beloved: therefore understand the matter, and consider the vision." [8]

Here we see, as it were, the fulfilment of the divine promise to Israel: "If my people, which are called by my name, shall humble themselves, and pray, and seek my face; ....then will I hear from heaven." [9] Daniel's prayer ascends to the throne of God; and at the beginning of his supplication, God gives the commandment to the angel Gabriel to bring the divine answer unto the greatly-beloved man, or the man of intense spiritual desire.

All these assurances of Scripture, illustrated by almost every great saint in Israel's history, from Abraham to Moses, to Samuel, to David, to Elijah, to Daniel, are brought before us with a still more intense brightness in the person, teaching, and example of the Lord Jesus. He is in all things the Mediator; prayer and answer to prayer are embodied in Him as their eternal Centre. He who is the way from man to God, and the way from God to man, is the prayer of God's children to the Father, and the Yea and Amen of God's promises to the children. He was a Man of prayer, and all His disciples knew that He was heard: "I know that, whatsoever Thou wilt ask of God, God will give it Thee." [10] In Jesus praying — in the distinct command of Jesus to pray, and to pray in His name — in His oft-repeated and most forcible assurances of the certain answer from God, the Scripture testimony concerning prayer reaches its culminating point; and it is from *this central light* that the Christian's experience of the reality of prayer must continually emanate and be renewed.

However true and valuable the reflection may be, that God, foreseeing and foreordaining all things, has also foreseen and foreordained our prayers as links in the chain of events, of sequences, of cause and effect, as a real power and influence, or viewed from the Christian's point, that prayer like faith is one of the covenant gifts and blessings; yet we feel convinced that this is not the light in which the mind can find peace on this great subject, nor do we think that here is the attractive power to draw us to prayer. We feel rather that such a reflection *diverts* the attention from the Object, whence alone comes the life, impulse, and strength of prayer. It may be a valuable thought after we have prayed and been heard, but it has no power to draw out prayer. The living God, cotemporary and not merely eternal — the loving, merciful, compassionate, righteous, and holy One — God manifesting Himself to the soul — God saying, "Give me, my son, thy heart;" or, "Ask what shall I give thee;" or, "Seek my face;" or, "Behold the Lamb of God," — this is the magnet that draws us — this alone can open heart and lips.

We may by careful explanation succeed in keeping such minds as are capable of such thoughts from mistaking our attempt to harmonize the eternal counsel of God and prayer, for the cold regions of dead and silent fatalism where there is no voice and no response. The Scripture method is entirely different; it connects prayer with the self-manifestation of the living God. The knowledge of God, as Father, Son, and Holy Ghost, is the root and foundation of prayer; the simple word, "God is love," the unanswerable argument against all doubts.

For we can only speak to a Person, to One living now, listening to us. Because God lived from all eternity, does He not live now? Because God has foreseen all things, does He not see this instant my need, my sorrow, my heart crying out for Him? Because there is no evil in the city but the Lord has foreseen it, and connected it with the development of His kingdom, and the manifestation of His character, is He not testifying to me against all evil, and willing and able to deliver me, nay, to be asked not to lead me into temptation? The highest idea of God, as revealed unto Israel, and at last in all its fulness in Jesus Christ, is connected with prayer. "God is Spirit," the Lord taught the woman of Samaria. "He seeth in secret," Jesus repeatedly says in the sermon on the mount. And what is the inference? God is Spirit, God is Father, and therefore He *seeks worshippers.* "He seeth in secret," and therefore prayer is delivered from all fetters and all limitations. Pray, and God hears. God forgives sin, He removes our transgressions, and clothes us with divine righteousness, in order that He may be worshipped." All that we know now of God is, that having removed all obstacles which were in the way, it is His will and delight that we should come to Him, that we should live in spiritual communion with Him — spiritual, that means real, inward, our very self speaking to Him, and living in His presence, Jesus therefore continually commands us to pray to the Father, who Himself, in spontaneous and infinite love, loveth us in time and in eternity.

In Jesus Christ, the Son of God and the Son of man, we have the full solution of the difficulty. He prayed on earth, and that not merely as man, but as the Son of God incarnate. His prayer on earth is only the manifestation, in His state of humiliation, of His prayer after His exaltation, and of His prayer from all eternity, when in the divine counsel He was set up as the Christ. The intercession of the Lord Jesus is based on His death, resurrection, and ascension. He is our Advocate, because He is our Righteousness. He is our Representative, because He is our Head, the last Adam. The Lord Jesus identifies Himself with us, and the Father regards Christ and the Church as one. Our prayers ascend with, through, and in Christ's prayer. Thus the Father hears only one voice, the voice of the Son, whom He heareth (answereth) alway. On the other hand, Jesus, identifying Himself with the Father, sends the Spirit into our hearts, so that we pray in the Spirit, according to God's will, in the name of Christ; we offer the very petitions which Jesus presents on our behalf.

But the intercession or prayer of the Son of God did not begin in time. We must conceive of it as eternal. Not merely did the saints of God before the advent draw near to God's throne through His mediation (more or less clearly apprehended), but He is the Beginning of the creation of God. He was appointed to be heir of all things. He is the Lamb foreordained from before the foundation of the world. All things were ordained and created for the manifestation of God's glory in Christ. And thus the Son of God was from all eternity the Mediator, the Way. He was, to use our imperfect language, from eternity speaking unto the Father on behalf of the world, on behalf of the manifestation of God's glory in His love. And the Father from all eternity hears the Son, gives unto Him, and is glorified in Him. [12]

God, in hearing His Son, heard only the echo of His own will. As we distinguish the persons, we hold fast the unity, of the Godhead. The Father's will and the Son's prayer are one; yet is the Son's prayer real; even as now Christ assures us that He prays for us; and again, to remind us of His oneness with the Father, He adds, "I say not, I will pray unto the Father; for the Father Himself loveth you."

There is no antagonism between prayer in time and the unchangeable will of God in eternity; for Christ — the Wisdom set up from everlasting; the *Word,* speaking unto God as well as out of God — is the bridge, the solution of all problems, the peaceful light in our darkness and exile.

Praying in the name of Christ, we pray according to the eternal purpose, according to the perfect will of God. We pray in perfect righteousness and liberty; for we are identified with Him who bore and took away our sins, thereby glorifying God, and bringing to us divine righteousness. We pray in newness of life; for in the resurrection of Christ, He became the quickening Spirit. We pray in the bright region of divine love, according to the Saviour's intercession, "that the love wherewith Thou hast loved Me may be in them, and I in them." [13]

The Holy Spirit, proceeding from the Father and the Son, is the Spirit of prayer. He is given unto us. He is sent into our hearts by the Feather, as the Spirit of His Son; and all He teaches us, and works in us, is summed up in this, that He cries in us, "Abba, Father;" that is, that by Him we realize, in a clear, fervent, and continuous manner, that we are the children of God in Christ Jesus. Hence to possess the Spirit is both the power and the object of all prayer. The Father gives the Spirit unto them that ask Him, because the Spirit is the sum of all good gifts. The promise of the Father — the culminating gift of the Lord Jesus glorified — the highest of all divine manifestations, He by whom the Father and the Son take up their abode in us — is the Spirit of grace and supplication. If the Spirit dwell in us, we pray without ceasing; in our infirmities we have an ever-present help — the lamp is continually renewed and cherished with the holy oil. In our most languid condition, when the soul cleaves to the dust. He maketh intercession for us, and God knoweth the mind of the Spirit in our sighs and groaning. Conscious of our ignorance and of our utter weakness, we change our very helplessness into a source of comfort; for the Spirit of all knowledge, power, and love is within us — our Paraclete. [14]

Thus the self-manifestation of God as Father, Son, and Holy Ghost, contains throughout the strongest and clearest call to prayer; and to know God as Father, to behold Him in Jesus, and to experience the communion of the Holy Spirit, is impossible without bowing the knee before the God and Father of our Lord, without invoking Christ, and learning to pray in His name, without the trustful and fervent prayer in the Holy Ghost. God lives, "God is Love," we therefore pray.

Let us consider now the same subject from the human point of view.

What is Christianity or religion? "Christianity does not leave us in a state of loneliness, only in communion with our own hearts; it is dependence on God, dependence acknowledged, believed, loved, cherished. When this humility lives in the heart, it speaks out of the heart; there is question and response, supplication and thanksgiving. Again, is Christianity confiding faith? Faith prays, seeking forgiveness of Him with whom it is. If Christianity implies virtue, benevolence, meekness, purity, faithfulness, it implies the fight of faith, and its ultimate strength is to take hold of omnipotence; it is prayer." [15]

Christianity is, above all, love. If we love, God dwelleth in us, and we in Him. Because "God is Love," He dispenses His gifts and blessings in such a manner as to draw us into the circle of love. In our salvation, Father, Son, and Holy Ghost work together in love and joy. The Father blesses us in the Son of His love, and rejoices over the sheep found and saved by the Good Shepherd. Jesus rejoices over us, as given unto Him of the Father. The Holy Ghost, who reveals to us the Father and the Son, sheds abroad in our hearts divine love. And now begins the prayer of love, love speaking both for ourselves and others; for God makes all believers workers together with Him. They are to be channels of His blessing to others, and the gifts, which He purposes to bestow, are first to be asked and prayed for by our loving hearts, that so we also may rejoice and give thanks for the abundant grace bestowed by the God of love.

> "More things are wrought by prayer
> Than this world dreams of..............
> For what are men better than sheep or goats,
> That nourish a blind life within the brain,
> If, knowing God, they lift not hands of prayer
> Both for themselves and those who call them friend?
> For so the whole round earth is every way
> Bound by gold chains about the feet of God."

Tennyson.

God, who cannot hide anything from the children of faithful Abraham, calling them friends, reveals to them not merely His counsel, but, giving them the loving Spirit of intercession, makes them sharers of His love and of His joy. [16] The angels also, who rejoice over every sinner that repenteth, and who minister unto the heirs of salvation, are associated with us in the golden circle of love, the centre of which is, and ever shall be, the Lamb of God, once slain, and now exalted on the throne to the glory of the Father,

To live before God, to meditate on His words and works, to ascribe glory to His name, revealed unto us now fully, is impossible without the transition of this state of realizing God into the act of prayer. Meditation and adoration are the necessary basis and element out of which prayer proceeds, and into which it returns. But they are not prayer. In prayer the soul concentrates all its energies, and appears before God, speaking to Him, and giving itself to Him in humility, repentance, trust, love, and childlike petitions for grace and strength, and all needful gifts. Wishes, cares, anxieties prepare the heart for prayer, [17] but are not prayer until they are converted into direct address, supplication, and cry unto God. Remembering with gladness the gracious invitations of God, who continually encourages us in our weakness, and reopens the sin-disturbed communion, this also is not prayer. It leads to prayer when we say to God, When Thou saidst unto me. Seek ye my face, my heart said unto Thee, Thy face, Lord, I will seek. [18]

In prayer we pass from the general to the individual, from contemplation to appropriation by the will, from the indirect He to the direct Thou. There is nothing more solemn, more difficult, [19] more glorious, than prayer; there is nothing, blessed be God, so easy, so accessible, so tenderly and sweetly implanted in us by divine grace.

We are accustomed to compare prayer with the breathing of the quickened soul now transplanted into the atmosphere of divine love and life; we may also compare it with eating, assimilating divine truths, promises, commands, so that they are appropriated by our hearts and wills, and converted into our spiritual life-strength. It is in prayer that we hear the word of God, and live by it.

It is the experience of the Christian, that through prayer he obtains light — insight into divine truths — which he could not gain by any other means. Natural power and penetration, the letter of Scripture and human instruction, have proved to be of no avail; we try to gain or force from without an entrance into the temple of truth. When we pray, God opens from within, and He gives unto us a knowledge which is not formal and abstract, but a vision and appropriation of realities. The Spirit, who knows our need, reveals unto us such truth, which we can assimilate, and which thus becomes nourishment to our spiritual life. Nor does it in the least lessen the reality of this divine answer to prayer, that the humble and expectant attitude prepares the mind, tranquillizes the heart, and purifies the soul, and that the asking must be followed by seeking and knocking. This Is doubtless true. Prayer is in harmony with all God's dealings, and with all the operations of the Spirit; but the light is sent *in answer to prayer*. The apostle Paul is so convinced of this, that he not merely writes the epistles according to the wisdom given unto him, but he tells the churches that he prays for them, that God may enlighten their minds, and give them spiritual understanding and knowledge. And so it is with all spiritual blessings. "Prayer brings all heaven before our eyes," and within our reach.

If we estimated rightly the relative magnitude of temporal and spiritual blessings, the relative difficulty of removing spiritual maladies and evils, and of delivering us from external ills, we should be more astonished at the marvels of divine grace, manifested in the answer to spiritual petitions. We are astonished when we hear of remarkable answers to prayer, in deliverance from sickness, from bodily danger, from outward distress and necessity. But how much more wonderful are the gifts of patience, meekness, fortitude, of persevering and forbearing love, of cheerfulness and diligence, of victory over besetting sins; or the secret and deep-reaching influences of the Spirit, calming the heart in anxiety, subduing the power of subtle and perplexing sin, upholding the soul with the joy of divine salvation! If the inward experience of the saints were known, if the journey through the Spirit-land could be described, how many marvellous answers to prayer would be seen — manna descending from heaven, rocks opening to send forth streams, guarding angels keeping us from falling over precipices and shielding us against the fiery darts of the wicked one! The outward answers to prayer strike us more for this, among other reasons, that we are not so conscious of our absolute dependence on God for every spiritual gift and deliverance, as we are at times of our absolute dependence on God for providential help and succour. Only be humble, and look back on your past life, and you will acknowledge how God has heard your prayer always and abundantly, else would you not be now where you are, a believer at the throne of grace.

Greater difficulties are felt with regard to petitions for *temporal* blessings, gifts, or deliverances.

The Christian feels that there is no desire, plan, or enterprise, no act and no relationship of life, in which he is not dependent on divine guidance, help, and blessing. He also feels that his relation of a child involves the confiding and unreserved love which pours out the whole heart before God, [20] And if we are to give thanks in everything, and do all things to the glory of God, how is it possible that any step or duty or activity of life should be excluded from our petitions? The only difficulty is in ourselves. God, without whose will not a sparrow falls to the ground, is willing and able to hear us in our most minute petitions, to guide and help us in all things. The reason we hesitate in offering such petitions is because we are not perfectly sure that what we desire is a real blessing, or that we desire it from a pure motive, or that our desire is in due relation to the one great aim of the Christian life. The difficulty is not whether it is right to ask for temporal things, but whether the things we desire are really good gifts, and whether in desiring them our hearts are right before God. We often mistake a stone for nutritious bread, and instead of a fish ask for a serpent, which would tempt us into evil. It is this consciousness which often cramps the Christian in prayer for earthly blessings. The importance of spiritual petitions is felt to be much greater, according to the command to seek first the kingdom of His righteousness, coupled with the promise, that all other things shall be added to us.

But, bearing these subjective difficulties in mind, let us not fall into the error of excluding from prayer what really occupies and interests us; for do we thereby avoid or decrease the danger of desiring wrong objects, and in a wrong way? Is not our only safety to bring our desires before God, to place them in the light of His countenance, to sift them on our knees, and see whether we can convert them into petitions? And what cannot be turned into petition can yet be brought before God, that He may correct and guide, that He may deliver us from self-will and fretful disappointment, that He may keep us in perfect peace. Thus our conviction that God doeth all things well, and our feeling, which is often tempted to doubt, murmur, and repine, will be brought into harmony. We notice this "parrhesia," speaking out all and pouring out our heart, with its fears and hopes, doubts and sorrows, murmuring and resistine. in the Psalms of David and in the prophets. Walking thus with God, answers to prayer in our daily life will continually be vouchsafed to us; nay, it may be said, that the more fully we are brought into spiritual communion with God, and the more we enter into the spirit of the prayer Christ gave us as a model, seeking first the divine and heavenly blessings, the more do we obtain the continual guidance and help we ask for our daily and earthly life.

The Scripture encouragements are very distinct. We are not to be overanxious about anything; but by prayer and supplication, with thanksgiving, make our requests known unto God. And how frequent and abundant are God's answers to our petitions for guidance and help in our life, even in its minute detail! [21] How does God connect the enjoyment of His presence, the assurance of His favour, and the desire for greater spiritual blessing, with the realized help from above in the ordinary duties and trials of our path! If our affections are set on things above, if our petitions are not a tempting of the Lord while we disregard His precepts, if in all our seeking we seek Him, then let no false spirituality or world-wisdom keep us from bringing before God all our thoughts and desires, plans and purposes, work and labour, fears and hopes — from speaking to Him as a child to his father

Let nothing shake our confidence. David often cried unto God, Why art Thou silent? Yet unless he had believed even then that God does hear and answer, he would not have persevered in prayer. The answer may be delayed to test our faith, to sift our motives, to prepare us for the right reception of the answer; but let us never doubt that whatsoever we ask in Christ's name will be granted unto us. And this faith, nothing wavering, is itself the test of the sincerity of our heart, and the Christ-conformed character of our petitions.

Prayer is not one among many manifestations of spiritual life; it is not even enough to say that it is the first and most important. It stands by itself, and pre-eminent. It is *the* manifestation of our personal relation to God; it is the essential and immediate expression of our filial relation in Christ to the Father. "Behold, he prayeth," is the beginning of the new life; "Abba, Father," is the first word of the regenerate. Here again we behold the unity and equality of all God's children. However weak their faith, knowledge, utterance, they can pray, they offer the soul's sincere desire; the Spirit Himself helpeth our infirmities. "The golden thread of prayer goes through the life of the just, excluding what is evil and false, and securing what is pure and good."

[1] Ps. cxxxix.
[2] Ps. xxxiii. 11.
[3] Eph. i. 11.
[4] Matt. vii. 7.
[5] I Kings iii. 5.
[6] Ps. l. 14.
[7] James i. 5.
[8] Dan. ix. 20-23.
[9] Chron. vii. 14.
[10] John xi. 22.
[11] Ps. cxxx. 4

[12] "We do not realize sufficiently the distinctness of the Persons in the unity of the Godhead. The eternal life of God is the communion of the Three blessed Ones; 'each divine Person' — to use the words of Schmieder — 'working in His peculiar sphere in original and creative glory that which the other Persons could not work and express in the same way.'" (*Hohepriesterliche Gebet.*) "Thus the Son spoke from all eternity to the Father, and the Father answered and gave; and herein is the Father's glory and joy, as well as the glory and joy of the Son. That there might be a glory given the Son from everlasting is clear from this, that there was the highest and freest mutual converse held between the Three Persons amongst themselves from everlasting, when no creature was; and in that converse they drove and carried on designs of what was to come, and gave the glory to one another, of what each of them was, or should be, or do, in their several activities, to all eternity. They spake one to another, and one of another, as Heb. x.: the Son of man said to the Father, 'A body hast Thou prepared Me;' and the Father to the Son, 'Thou art my Son; this day have I begotten Thee.' And this latter was from everlasting, in the decreeing of it, spoken to Him; for the words spoken before are, '*I will declare the decree.*' Whereof that speech therefore was the matter. Likewise there were mutual engagements and promises passed between them. (Titus i. 1, 2.) Eternal life was promised afore the world began; and there must be an intercourse of persons promising, and that received and ac-

cepted the promise. And in like manner in their converses they glorified one another. *'The Spirit shall glorify Me,'* says Christ. (John xvi. 14.) He says it indeed of His glorifying Christ to us; but if He doeth it to us, much more among themselves." — *Goodwin on the Knowledge of God.*

[13] Compare my *Lord's Prayer,* chap. i.: "Prayer as revealed in Christ."

[14] "The prayers I make will then be sweet indeed,
    If Thou the Spirit give by which I pray;
    My unassisted heart is barren clay,
    That of its native self can nothing feed;
    Of good and pious works Thou art the seed,
    That quickens only where Thou say'st it may.
    Unless Thou shew to us Thy own true way,
    No man can find it. Father! Thou must lead.
    Do Thou, then, breathe those thoughts into my mind,
    By which such virtue may in me be bred,
    That in Thy holy footsteps I may tread;
    The fetters of my tongue do Thou unbind,
    That I may have the power to sing to Thee,
    And sound Thy praises everlastingly."   Wordsworth.

[15] Nitzsch.

[16] Abraham's intercession for the cities of the plain illustrates the spirit of truth and love which characterizes God's children. Luther says: "Six times he intercedes, with such earnestness and heartfelt yearning, that in his great anguish and desire he utters almost foolish words. But it is a most precious prayer, if you judge of it by the attitude of his heart; for it was a very violent emotion and profound importunity. There was more in the holy man's heart than that heart could understand and feel. I am sure tears ran down his face, and his words passed into unspeakable sighs."

[17] The promises are not given to our *wants,* but to our *petitions.* — Whately.

[18] Ps. xxvii. 8.

[19] "Believe me," said Coleridge to his nephew, two years before his death, "to pray with all your heart and strength, with the reason and the will, to believe vividly that God will listen to your voice through Christ, and verily do the thing He pleaseth thereupon — this is the last, the greatest achievement of the Christian's warfare upon earth. Teach us to pray, Lord." — *Coleridge's Table-talk.*

[20] "This is the blessed privilege of speaking out our heart to God. We know from the outset that we are wrong. We do not doubt that God will do what is right; yet we feel our breast oppressed. And to whom else can we go but to our Lord, the eternal and living God?" — Zinzendorf.

[21] Rothe, in his very valuable exposition of this subject (Ethic iii. 498), quotes the remarks of Reinhard: "It must excite the attention of every thoughtful person, that the belief, God hears prayer, is found among all nations who have a knowledge of Deity, and is fundamentally peculiar to the whole human race. There must be a greater number of experiences of answers to prayer than is generally supposed, else the belief in the utility of prayer would not be so general, vivid, and prevalent." The experiences of Francke, W. Huntington (*Bank of Faith*), and George Müller, are most instructive and encouraging.

Chapter Seven - God Draws Nigh in Consolation

"Draw nigh to God, and He will draw nigh to you." - James iv. 8.

There is only one thing which we can secure on earth, which we can obtain with absolute certainty and keep with perfect security. All other things which we may desire and seek we can only obtain partially, and then their possession is most insecure, and at best only for a short season. The only thing which we can most absolutely and certainly gain on earth is heaven. It is the only thing, and at the same time the highest, the best — life and blessedness everlasting. There is only one thing which every one that seeketh is sure to find. There is only one thing which, when once found, can never be taken from us. It is the love of God which is in Christ Jesus our Lord; it is Jesus Himself, the Son of God, the Pearl of great price.

As there is only one thing we can secure on earth, it is only on earth we can secure this one thing. Unless we gain Christ, our earthly life is a total and irreparable failure. How solemn and how sweet is the gospel-message! It is the offer of a gift, without which we are lost. The gift is Jesus. We can never receive any gift equal to or like Him to all eternity. The most marvellous experience of the love of God is here on earth, when we believe in Jesus. God Himself draws nigh to us with the assurance of His eternal and immutable love. Christ is ours — wisdom, righteousness, sanctification, and redemption — and the sinner, who but a moment before was poor and sad, is able to rejoice in unsearchable riches, and to glory in God.

When we have once experienced the love of God in Christ Jesus, we cannot but draw nigh continually, that God may draw nigh to us. Having tasted that the Lord is gracious, we desire the sincere milk of the Word, that we may grow thereby. We know now that our Father in heaven has *only* good gifts to give to His children. We are not afraid of the word of God, although it is sharper than a two-edged sword. Our God is a consuming fire, and yet we draw nigh with the confiding and joyous expectation of abundant and peaceful blessings. "I will hear," saith the believer, "what God the Lord will say: for He will speak *peace* to His people, and to His saints." How blessed the assurance, that whatever God says. He speaks *peace!* In all His rebukes and chastenings, the thoughts of His heart concerning us are *peace*. Scripture is nothing else but consolation, [1] beginning with the poor in spirit and the contrite mourners, and accompanying us to the very end of our earthly pilgrimage.

God comforts, comforts His people, and speaks to the heart of Jerusalem. [2] To the soul, turning away from sin and earth, He has only consolation; in the valley of the shadow of death His staff and His rod comfort us, and beyond the grave we behold Lazarus is comforted, and God Himself wipes away all tears from the eyes of His children.

The consolations of God, sweet and lovely as they are to the new man, are bitter and piercing to the old Adam nature. Jesus is the consolation of Israel, and Jesus is a Saviour from sin. Jesus is not of this world; Jesus was crucified that sin might be condemned in the flesh. The Holy Ghost is the Comforter, and, as the very name indicates, the Spirit, who in His infinite love condescends to dwell in our hearts, in whom the Father and the Son draw nigh, even so nigh as to take up their abode within us, is holy, separating us from all sin and worldliness. Are we willing to be comforted by God, in Jesus, through the Holy Ghost? Have we courage, let me rather say faith, to be filled with divine light and love? Have we resolved to give up all things, nay, to hate our own lives, that *God* may draw nigh to us? Then let not our hearts be troubled; the Lord, whose love is infinite in majesty, wisdom, power, and tenderness, saith, "I, even I, am He that comforteth you." [3]

We need consolation throughout our whole course. This may seem strange at first. As without Christ there is not a single gleam of light to break our darkness, so with Christ there ought not to be a single cloud on our horizon, no doubt or fear to interrupt the peace which His precious blood has purchased for us. Under the law there was nothing but condemnation; under the gospel there is nothing but the all-sufficient Saviour-grace of God. Yet what is our experience?

The soul asks, Why have I such a constant and painful remembrance of past, of forgiven sin? It is true that all prophets and apostles testify of Jesus, that in Him is forgiveness of sins to every one that believeth. Even to the little children the beloved apostle writes, because their sins are forgiven for His name's sake. In all the Pauline epistles the believer is assured that in Christ we have, we possess, redemption, even the forgiveness of sins; that this is the fundamental blessing of the new covenant; that God hath forgiven our iniquities, and will remember our sins no more. God has assured us that He has blotted out our sins as a thick cloud, that He has removed them from us as far as the east is from the west, that He has buried them in the depths of the sea, and that this perfect and absolute forgiveness is that in which He delights, and wherein He manifests to all angels and ages His glory. And yet we cannot forget our past sins, and we feel the need to be constantly reassured by the voice saying, "Take, eat; this is my body, broken for you: this is my blood, shed for the remission of sin," Why is this?

When we first returned to God we had very shallow and limited views of the nature of sin, of the depth of the fall, of the hidden alienation of the carnal mind from God. Our heavenly Father, in His loving-kindness and tenderness, allowed us then to experience chiefly the sweetness of His mercy. We rejoiced in the bright robe, in the ring of adoption, in the shoes of the new obedience, in the joy of the Good Shepherd, who had found His lost sheep. God blessed us, and assured us of His never-changing love. But it is necessary that we should learn more of sin, in order that we may continue to rest *exclusively* on Christ. If the atoning blood of Jesus is to remain our only trust, if the indwelling of Christ by the Spirit is to be our only strength, it is necessary that we should know and remember our sins, that we should feel them painfully, and be ashamed before God. It is after the brethren of Joseph are pardoned, it is after Israel has experienced the marvellous love of God, that the sense of sin, the overwhelming and crushing sense of sin, is felt. "Thou son of man," said God to the prophet Ezekiel, "shew the house to the house of Israel, that they may be ashamed of their iniquities." [4] The completeness and glory of the temple call forth the deepest repentance.

Let no man think the believer's sighs the language of unbelief, or his tears the expression of unconsoled sorrow. Let no presumptuous hand remove the bitter herbs from the paschal feast. It is a great forgiveness which God bestows, which Jesus purchased, which the Spirit seals, and we *feel* it to be *great*. And as we feel God's forgiveness great, so we cannot forget that all our sins, though forgiven, are still within us. They are blotted out, they are judged, they are crucified; we hate them, we fight against them; but there they are, within us, ours. Our whole old man, with all its members, is still in *existence*. Grace has not annihilated him, although grace enables us to crucify him, to mortify the members which are on earth. How can we help remembering what we were, and what we did, when sin, although no longer reigning within us, is still present with us, when the flesh still, daily and always, is in mortal enmity against the Spirit. Poor believer! wretched man! chief of sinners! God will comfort thee. How often dost thou cry —

"Say this word of love again,
Christ receiveth sinful men!"

How often does thy soul respond —

"Chief of sinners though I be,
Christ is all in all to me!"

Believe and rejoice in the Lord. "Worthy is the Lamb." Say not merely, "I am black;" but behold the beauty of the Lord.

"Your many sins are all forgiven;
Oh, hear the voice of Jesus!
Go on your way in peace to heaven,
And wear a crown with Jesus."

The soul mourns over her many sins, and the fewness of her good works. She thinks grace hath won but scanty triumphs; she wonders why sin is not extirpated; she is disappointed that the heavenly Gardener does not remove the bitter root of sins; she has sometimes imagined for days and weeks that He had done so. A subtle and sweet calm, an unwonted energy as of the Spirit, a Sabbatic freedom from the attacks of old sins and habits, seemed to descend into the soul; she felt herself pure, beautified, no longer in the wilderness, always victorious. Alas! it was Satan appearing as an angel of light. Jesus Christ, the crucified, the Physician of the sick, the Healer of the broken-hearted, the Saviour of sinners, is not the centre and root of this experience. This sweetness and honey come not from the cleft Rock.

God's thoughts are not our thoughts; His ways are not our ways. We discover this continually. Not merely when we are first brought to a knowledge of salvation, and see with rejoicing surprise the marvellous method of free grace, but ever afterwards we learn that the ways of God are different from our wisdom and the expectation of our hearts. How natural is the thought and desire of the soul that has begun to love Christ, that its progress may now be continuous and rapid! How natural even the conception, that in some moment of faith and ardent soul-surrender, there will be given from above a complete and final victory over the love of sin and the world! Yet how different is the experience of the Christian! Is it not true of all, what an old saint describes as his history? —

"I ask'd the Lord that I might grow
 In faith and love, and ev'ry grace;
 Might more of His salvation know,
 And seek more earnestly His face.

"'Twas He who taught me thus to pray,
 And He, I trust, has answer'd prayer;
 But it has been in such a way,
 As almost drove me to despair.

"I hoped that in some favour'd hour
 At once He'd answer my request,
 And by His love's constraining power
 Subdue my sins, and give me rest.

"Instead of this, He made me feel
 The hidden evils of my heart;
 And let the angry powers of hell
 Assault my soul in every part.

"Yea, more; with His own hand he seem'd
 Intent to aggravate my woe;
 Cross'd all the fair designs I schem'd,
 Blasted my gourds, and laid me low.

"'Lord, why is this?' I trembling cried;
 'Wilt Thou pursue thy worm to death?'
 ''Tis in this way,' the Lord replied,
 'I answer prayer for grace and faith.

"'These inward trials I employ,
 From self and pride to set thee free;

And break thy schemes of earthly joy,
   That thou mayst seek thy all in Me.'"

The heavenly wisdom speaks to us in this wise: God has commanded us to fight the good fight of faith as long as we are on earth; the city of palm trees is beyond; vision and strifeless joy await us in the heavenly Jerusalem. Our rest is in God even now; but it is not the rest of glory. The old man is not annihilated in us, else were there no conflict. Do we wish to be pure and faultless, in order to give the glory to God? If suddenly our sin was removed, would we ascribe it to God, and to God alone? And though we should say so with our lips, would not our secret thoughts be, My idol hath done this? would not the enemy whisper it to our heart? Have we not often experienced how a smooth and outwardly faultless and peaceful course only concealed a disease more dangerous and more loathsome — the sin of hard, self-contained and self-satisfied Pharisaism, which needs no Saviour, and has no tears of joy, gratitude, and shame to shed? [5] We cannot be too earnest, diligent, and watchful; we cannot have too high an aim, and too hopeful a trust in the strength of Jesus.

It is an essential feature in the Christian, that he longs after holiness. Sanctification is inseparably connected with justification, not only as its companion, but its end. "If we compare them in point of time, if we look backward, holiness was always necessary unto happiness; or if we look forward, the estate we are appointed to, and for which we are delivered from wrath, is an estate of perfect holiness." [6] If we look to the eternal election of the Father, if we reflect upon the great work of redemption, if we by faith realize the fulfilment of the promise, and behold the new Jerusalem, into which nothing shall enter that is defiled, everywhere we see holiness as the great object of the divine purpose and the divine acts of grace. Again, every privilege of the Christian points to this great end. Are we the children of God? Then the command follows naturally: "Be ye holy; for I am holy." "Be ye therefore perfect, even as your Father which is in heaven is perfect." "Be ye followers (imitators) of God, as dear children." Are we the disciples of Christ? Then it is ours to learn of Him, who was meek and lowly in heart. Are we His friends? Then it is for us to do whatsoever He commands us. Are we members of the Church, of the body of which the Son of God is Head? Then is it for us to walk worthy of the vocation wherewith we are called, and to remember that the Holy Ghost Himself dwelleth in us.

As the desire after holiness [7] is an essential feature in the Christian character, and constant sorrow and conflict on account of sin — our worst, and in one sense our only, enemy — the mark of every true believer, so the desire after a state of perfection and completeness is also well founded; only that here misconceptions easily creep in, especially if they flatter our self-complacency, and give room to glory in ourselves. We are complete in Christ. We receive in Jesus, once and for ever, all things pertaining to life and godliness. We are by faith one with Him, whom God has made for us wisdom and righteousness, sanctification and redemption. Jesus, the ascended Lord, is our perfection. As our righteousness is in heaven, as the name both of the Lord and of Jerusalem is Jehovah-Tsidkenu, so is our perfection Christ at the right hand of God. And our hope is, that we shall be like Him; that when Jesus comes again we shall be, in body, soul, and spirit, conformed to the image of God's Son, according to the working whereby He is able to subdue all things unto Himself.

The Christian is at peace; he possesses in the present all he needs; he does not look forward to a gradual and slow progress, and to an indefinite goal, but to a constantly-renewed apprehension and enjoyment of what, by God's grace and through faith, has been given unto him in Christ Jesus.

There are three subjects of which the Christian has an experimental and real knowledge l sin, grace, and the new life and walk in Christ..

1. He has knowledge of sin, partly by self-observation and experience, but chiefly through faith in the testimony of God. Examining his thoughts, feelings, words, and actions, he cannot fail to discover pride, self-seeking, covetousness, and other evils within his heart. Sometimes sins, which he fancied he detested, will, to his great shame and terror, appear in his own heart; and evils, which he thought he had conquered and laid aside, are felt to have only slumbered to assert themselves with new and greater power.

But however humiliating such discoveries are, it is not in this way that we arrive at a true knowledge and conviction of sin; it is by believing what God says of us in His word. If we measure our sinfulness by our own discovery and experience of it, we may indeed be deeply abased, but we do not see our condition in the true light. When we bow to the declaration of God's word — when we accept the testimony of Scripture, the estimate of divine justice, holiness, and truth — when we receive the judgment of Him, who searcheth and trieth the heart, then it is that we see and know ourselves to be sinners. Once we have accepted the divine testimony concerning sin, we retain this conviction of our sinfulness, even while we have the most comforting and encouraging experiences of divine favour. We know that Christ Jesus saved sinners, we also know "of whom I am chief."

The Scripture portraiture and anatomy of the human heart (as for instance Rom. iii. 10-18) may appear at first sight to be not merely appalling, but inapplicable in its full extent to our own case. If we measure it by our own feeling and experience, we may find it difficult to submit ourselves to the divine judgment, and to acknowledge its justice; but if we accept it in faith, if we remember that it is the sentence of God, of the Omniscient One, whose eyes are as a flame of fire, and whose word is perfect, we shall then, also in our experience and feeling, come to the knowledge of the truth of the Scripture declaration of our sinfulness. We shall then attribute to prevenient and restraining grace our comparative freedom from some of the manifestations of sin; we shall learn "that what is born of the flesh is flesh." Though we have not always the conscious *feeling* of our guilt and sin, yet, if we believe God's word, we always *know* ourselves to be sinners, and therefore are able always to rejoice in Jesus, who "receiveth sinners, and eateth with them."

2. In like manner our knowledge of Jesus, or of grace, is not according to our feeling, but according to the testimony which God has given of His Son. When we come to Jesus, we receive Him *at once, as He is,* in all His fulness, as God hath made Him for us;" we receive the whole Christ. The moment we are enabled to give our heart unto Jesus, we possess all; we are blessed with all spiritual blessings in heavenly places in Him. The believer is gradually growing in the knowledge and enjoyment of the blessings he has received; but the *possession* of them is not a gradual acquisition, but an immediate and perfect reception. The word of God declares that, believing in Jesus, I have *eternal life*. This is far beyond my conception, experience, and feeling; yet I believe and rejoice in this wonderful gift of life eternal. The peace of the Christian is perfect, because he possesses a perfect Christ.

3, And in like manner we have perfection and completeness in the spirit and character of our walk. The Christian's new life is not a gradual reception of isolated precepts and commandments, an isolated and mechanical exercise of individual virtues and self-denials, but the putting on of the new man; so that the mind which was in Christ Jesus is in us. By the death of Christ we have been crucified unto sin and the world. Sin in its totality has been condemned in the flesh. We, who believe on Jesus, have died unto sin with and in Him. Our whole life has sprung out of the resurrection of Christ. The one motive of our actions is, "We live not unto ourselves, but unto Him, who loved us, and gave Himself for us." The more we remember this completeness and unity of the "mind of Christ," into which we have entered by faith in the death and resurrection of our Lord, the more shall we be prepared and strengthened to overcome every temptation, to fulfil every duty, to solve every doubtful case, as it arises. The Christian's life and obedience is thus something complete, an organic whole. [9]

To sum up: if we are God's children, our experience will be, I must decrease, Christ must increase. Yet we grow. We are humbled, and yet we rise. God comforts us, that He will perform the work which He has begun in our souls, that He will perfect that which concerneth us, that we shall mount up with wings as eagles. And God's consolations give us perfect peace while we remain a poor afflicted people.

"Lowly, my eyes, be lowly!
   God from His throne above
Looks down upon the humble
   In kindness and in love.
Still as I rise I shall
   Have greater depths below me,
And haughty works must fall:
   Therefore, my eyes, be lowly."

Out of the depths we look to our true joy. As the children sing —

"Oh, how happy we shall be;
For our Saviour we shall see
Exalted on His throne! Oh, that will be joyful!"

We have a foretaste of this heavenly joy when it pleases God to give us a deep sense of our sin and unworthiness. To think of our sin and nothingness *leads* to humility. The true humility is to think with joy of Christ, and to magnify our God and Saviour. In the sweet valley of humiliation we behold Jesus exalted on His throne. Then the happy land, far, far away, seems very nigh; for we see the King in His beauty; our eyes behold the land that is far off. When we can truly say, "Christ is all," then God enables us to add, "And Christ is mine." When we have no righteousness of our own — when we can find nothing within ourselves wherein to trust and rejoice — when, more deeply and painfully than at our conversion, we feel our exceeding sinfulness and helplessness — then God comforts us with His abundant mercy; we behold the amazing, infinite, and immutable love of God; we rejoice with joy unspeakable and full of glory. Jesus Himself is our Righteousness, our Beauty. We sing the new song. God Himself is our Light and our Salvation.

The fulness and sweetness of divine love can be seen and felt by the soul, only when emptied and abased. There are only two heavens — one above in glory, the other below in the broken heart. When it is perfectly still within, when every voice of self-commendation or excuse is hushed, then is heard the voice of the Lord, full of majesty and consolation. God reveals His presence, God manifests His love, and we adore.

See, the frail bark is far away from the shore of time and sense; no longer are the hills of this earth within view; the last thin line of the coast has disappeared from the vision; the soul is alone with God. The ocean is infinite, and it is love. He loved us ere the foundations of the world were laid. We look no more for works of righteousness which we have done. Chosen in Christ, redeemed with His most precious blood, we know ourselves loved with a love which is its own source, which ever sustains and renews itself, and which brings us all that pertains to life and godliness.

Here is the true Sabbath of the soul. Ceasing from our works, from all spiritual labour and anxiety, we rejoice in Christ Jesus with the simplicity of little children. As in our earthly life, when we are far from the noise and dust of crowded streets, in some distant lonely spot, the deep, still, virgin silence makes us forget the burden of our daily routine, and there returns to us the freshness and fragrance of our childhood, so is it sometimes given to the Christian to return to his first love, and to the first Christ-absorbed adoring joy.

We are then in the Spirit. Is it *above?* As Moses was on the mount, high above the people, above the darkness of Sinai and the clouds of earth, and beheld the blue of heaven at the feet of the God of Israel, so is the soul lifted above the crowd of thoughts, accusing and excusing one another, and the works of the law, and the earthly imperfect willing and doing, and beholds the covenant faithfulness of everlasting love. Or is it *within?* Eyes and ears are closed; reason, fancy, and all energies of the soul rest in quiet expectation. The heavenly Friend has gently opened the door, and in the heart is heard His salutation: "Peace be with thee. Comfort ye, comfort ye my people, saith your God. Speak to the heart of Jerusalem, and say unto her that her warfare is accomplished, that her iniquity is pardoned, that she hath received of the Lord's hand a Benjamin-portion for all her sins."

[1] "Christianity does not bring consolation only in part or at the end, but it is consolation-doctrine from the beginning and throughout to the end; altogether it is organized consolation. Jesus begins with pronouncing the poor and mourners blessed. He is regarded by prophets and apostles as the day-spring of mercy." — Nietzsche, *Seelenpflege,* p. 173.

[2] Isa. xi. 2, orig.

[3] "There is no truth, however warning, threatening, yea, even terrifying, its aspect, which does not bring us nearer consolation, though apparently removing it from us. How faithful and truthful is the truth, which aims at our liberty and blessedness, that it takes from us step by step all false consolation, and in such a manner, that though at first we do not feel thankful, yet at last we must offer praise and adoration for this very discipline." — Nietzsche, *Seelenpflege,* p. 175.

[4] Ezek. xxxvi. 31; xliii. 10.

[5] The following extract is from the diary of Philip M. Hahn (Feb. 8th, 1786): "During my private prayer I remembered my impatient speech to-day, and this brought before me my sins in so clear a light, and with a deep feeling of sorrow and abhorrence. It showed me so clearly the necessity of an atonement, and the greatness of God's mercy, and that we live entirely by the grace of God, and are unworthy. I thought within myself, How necessary are our failures! For I know from experience that when some considerable time has passed without open failure, I become proud, unmerciful, self-complacent, censorious. One does not recognize God's mercy and compassion, and that God delights only in a childlike, humble heart. But this is by no means to encourage us in carelessness. It is to my shame that I have not the mind of Christ," &c. This remark, rightly understood, does not contradict the frequently-expressed exhortation of Scripture: "These things write we unto you, *that ye sin not.*"

[6] Archbishop Leighton.

[7] Dr. Duncan somewhere expresses doubt as to whether there is in the present day as much real anxiety and honest striving after assurance of faith, as interest in the discussion of the subject. Let us hope there is much real and sincere heart-longing for holiness, and for a close walk with God. The Scriptures contain simple and ample directions to all who wish to abide in Christ and bring forth fruit.

[8] I Cor. i. 30.

[9] Condensed from Steinhofer, who adds:

1. "If we are frequently attacked by the same sin, and fight against it, by itself, without going to the root of our being Christ's, and of our possessing the mind of Christ constantly indwelling, we are worsted, and become faint and without power.

2. "A believer has sinned, he perceives the defect, and he wishes to remedy the matter by feeling anxious, and by humble and sorrowful supplication for mercy (which is certainly right); but he fails to take his refuge in the strong tower of the Atonement. He does not remember that his sins are forgiven him; then he shall experience that 'the *law is the strength of sin.*'" He has returned to the stand-point of law, in which there is neither peace nor power.

Chapter Eight - If God Be For Us

"Draw nigh to God, and He will draw nigh to you." - James iv. 8.

There is no exhortation more solemn and profound, more fundamental, reaching" into the very beginnings of spiritual life, and more comprehensive, embracing the deepest experience of divine grace, than these words: "Draw nigh to God, and He will draw nigh to you." No frequency of repetition can weaken their force or exhaust their meaning; but they grow in power and sweetness as we obey the command, "Draw nigh to God," and test the truth of the promise, "And He will draw nigh to you."

You who are still far from Him, do you not know that He is? and knowing that He is, can you resist the magnet of almighty love, manifested in human sorrow, in Jesus lifted up to the cross? You hear the word of God; but do you not know that the word of God lives because *God lives?* You hear the invitations of divine grace; but do you not realize that God sends them forth, and that this moment there are the outstretched arms of Fatherly love ready to receive you? You hear the ambassadors of Christ; but have you never looked through them unto the heavenly throne, where Christ lives, exalted a Prince and a Saviour, to give repentance and remission of sins? "Draw nigh to God."

How long will you draw nigh to things which cannot draw nigh to you, to the creature which cannot even understand, far less satisfy, the depth of your thirst, or heal your conscience, or give you the peace which only an infinite love can bestow? How long will you allow sin, or the world, or the force of dull habit, to prevent you from facing the solemn realities of your eternal life, from turning unto the living God? And you who are satisfied with the *shadow* of Christ flitting across your mind and imagination, who rest in the knowledge of doctrine, and the theory of religion, "draw nigh to God," rend your hearts, repent and believe on the Lord Jesus Christ, and your sins shall be blotted out, and Jesus Himself shall dwell in your hearts. See, the poor and guilty one hears the call, "Draw nigh." Between the cherubim, on the blood-besprinkled mercy-seat, is the presence of the sin-forgiving and yet holy God; but the sinner stands afar off; an overwhelming awe, fear, shame, self-condemnation, transfix him to the ground. He cannot advance; he cannot draw nigh; he has no strength, no courage; he would not lift up so much as the eyes, the expression of hope and entreaty, to heaven. Upon his breast he smites; for he knows his sins came not from without, but from the depth of his own heart. So still is he, and absolutely poor. Behold, he has drawn nigh to God, and God has drawn nigh to him! [1]

Not in dark symbol, not in partial and fragmentary types, has God spoken to us. Who of us is ignorant of the name of Jesus? Who of us has not heard from childhood the sweet story of old? Unto whom is the image new of the Good Shepherd who laid down His life for the sheep, and whose greatest joy it is to seek and to save the lost one? And when the thought of judgment and eternity alarms the worldly heart, is it not the thought of God, who was in Christ, and who sent the message of reconciliation to His enemies? [2] It is not the remembrance of mount Sinai, but of Golgotha, which alarms the conscience in the prospect of death.

Oh, how near is God! The Word is nigh unto thee [3] — in thy mouth and in thy mind, in thy imagination and in thy conscience. Let it sink still deeper, where alone it can effect its grand object. *Believe with the heart in Jesus.* Faith is the opening of the heart to the love of God. "Draw nigh to God."

God draws nigh, only to comfort". The consolations of God have their centre in the cross of the Lord Jesus; but there is no human sorrow which they cannot reach, and no wound of the heart which they cannot heal.

Many, who do not feel the burden of sin, pass by Jesus, because they imagine He has nothing else to give but pardon. And it is true, that only through the forgiveness of sins all divine blessings descend into our hearts. But what Jesus has to give us, and He alone, is all that which we need. He possesses the only remedy for poor and weary humanity. He alone can give peace and health to the sick and restless heart. He calls to Himself all the heavy-laden and weary ones: "If any man thirst!"

For it is not a question about sin only, it is a question about myself. Man, who is not at peace with God, is not at peace with himself. Man lost many blessings, gifts, and treasures, many joys and hopes, when he departed from God. But above all, he lost himself when he forsook God. *He is* lost — *he*, and not merely what he once possessed. The centre of human existence is either outside us— in those whom we love, in activity and success in the world — or within us. "My mind to me a kingdom is, my self-approbation, my character." But from neither of these centres can peace and happiness flow into the soul. Created in the image of God, we have not lost the *thirst*, though we have departed from the fountain of living water. We are all seeking 'goodly' pearls. Alas! many receive and try to be satisfied with *their* good things, as we read of the rich man; [4] but all saints in heaven, and all lost ones in hell, testify that there is only *One* genuine, true, beautiful, and precious Pearl — the only One, all-comprehensive, all-sufficient, and eternal.

Men will never truly thank God for their creation until they praise Him for their redemption. Men must feel overwhelmed with the darkness of Providence until, inscribed upon the cross, they read, in shining letters, "God is love." A threefold pain takes hold of our souls when we realize the irreparable Past, with its errors, sins, and losses; the unsatisfying Present, with its emptiness and weary agitation; and the dark Future, with its uncertainty and gloom; [5] until we turn to that eternal love, which, with the bright eye of all-comprehensive wisdom and the tender hand of unfailing omnipotence, orders all things to work together for our good; unless we look to Jesus Christ, the same yesterday, to-day, and for ever; unless we draw nigh to God, and God draws nigh to us.

Do we know from experience this mysterious reciprocity and communion? Here is the true, the real life. There is a hidden life of thoughts and feelings in every man, and even this inner life is full of mysteries which we cannot fathom. But the Christian's hidden life is the life which is not merely hid in his own soul, but which is hid with Christ in God. It has two sanctuaries — one in heaven, one in the heart. It is dialogue, and not monologue; it is the continuous approach of God to the soul, and of the soul to God; it is the uninterrupted manifestation of Christ to the heart, and the constant response of adoration and love; it is the constant inworking of divine grace, and the constant outworking of the believer in willing and doing; it is the Spirit indwelling, witnessing, comforting, Christ-conforming; and our spirit, thus energized, taking hold of the Father and His Son Jesus Christ.

Say not that all I have described amounts simply to our praying to God, and to our receiving God's answer through the written Word. Surely prayer and the written Word are of essential importance. But drawing nigh to God means rather the essence and the culminating-point of prayer than prayer itself; it is that prayer which does not seek so much separate gifts of His grace, but which seeks to take hold of Himself. We ask not light, but that God should be our light; we ask not for pardon, but we desire to be kissed by the Father; we ask not holiness, but that the Holy One should dwell in our hearts and lives. We come to God; and in like manner, God Himself draws near unto us. Herein is the exceeding love of God, that His gifts and graces are not separate from Himself, but are part of His life within us. For the Father and the Son dwell in us by the Holy Spirit, [6] and thus we understand and possess in fulness what the Psalmist rejoiced in of old, that God Himself *is* our refuge and strength, our salvation and glory, the strength of our heart, and our portion for ever. It is the constant desire of the Christian thus to realize the indwelling of God. He speaks unto us as truly as He did unto Abraham, Moses, Paul. For we know that the revelations of God to them, the divine promises and commands, could be received only by faith. Peculiar and fundamental as are these revelations recorded in Scripture, yet are they not anomalous and isolated, but rather typical of all the self-manifestations of God to His chosen people.

Jesus gives unto us as immediate, all-sufficient, heart-convincing manifestation of Himself, as when He appeared unto the disciples, and said, "Peace be with you;" as when His condescending grace caused Thomas to cry out, "My Lord and my God;" as when He sent forth His deeply-tried and well-nigh despairing apostle with the assurance, "My grace is sufficient for thee." After

His resurrection our adorable Lord manifested Himself to His disciples. He who in the days of His flesh taught daily in the temple, and was seen and heard of the multitude, appeared now only unto His chosen friends. "God," as the apostle Peter says, "raised Him up the third day, and showed Him openly; not to all the people, but unto witnesses chosen before." He appeared. He drew near, He made Himself known. He afterwards called Saul by name, and revealed unto him His grace and power. The manifestation of the risen Saviour to His chosen ones, as recorded in Scripture, is typical of the dealings of the ascended Christ with the soul throughout this dispensation. It is the Lord Himself who appears, who speaks, who makes Himself known unto the heart. Mary Magdalene often seeks Him in great anxiety. Her intense anxiety partly prevents her recognising the presence of the beloved Master; but when He calls her by name, she knows it is He. The salutation, "Peace be with you," is heard, and, after sorrow and darkness, the sweet light shines again. And as in the instances recorded in the gospels, the Saviour honours the written Word in the most marked manner, connecting it in an inseparable manner with Himself, His work, and His self-manifestation, so in all the subsequent experiences of the church Christ reveals Himself in, with, and by the Word, and yet in such a manner that it is known *He* reveals Himself. The written Word is indeed the pre-eminent and, in many ways, indispensable and unique channel; but it is God Himself who draws nigh to the heart drawing nigh to Him.

Here and here only is peace and consolation. Seek it not in doctrines skilfully and soothingly-arranged to give you calm slumber and a kind of logical and legal trust-deed security; seek it only in and from the living God. "I, even I, am He that comforteth you." It is a divine prerogative. Thus God says often emphatically, "I, even I," to exclude all idols, however beautiful and elevated — to shut us up to Himself. God alone created the heavens and the earth — "I, even I;" God alone redeemed us, and forgiveth all our iniquities — "I, even I;" God alone, who knows the heart, can heal and gladden it.

And as God draws nigh to comfort us in our sorrow for sin, so it is His manifested presence which alone can comfort us in affliction, and amid the various difficulties of our earthly life.

The soul is troubled because of errors and self-chosen paths, which have brought to us trial and disappointment. We feel that our own mistakes, wrong decisions, and culpable yielding to worldly and sinful influences have borne bitter fruit. While we fear that we have thus marred and injured our future, and while with bitter regret we dwell on the past, we feel that it would involve much self-abasement to draw nigh unto the Lord, that His presence might bring us, above all, inward calm, and afterwards deliverance. When our own conduct has converted a brother into an adversary, and the homeward path into a dangerous journey, we feel like Jacob, near a severe conflict. [7] But when God draws nigh. He, it is true, begins the conflict with us; [8] but how wonderful is the victory which by His own grace we gain! For we draw nigh to God, and He to us. The soul says: "Peniel: I have seen *God* face to face, and my life is preserved."

Or, in seasons of affliction and bereavement, in times of difficult and perplexing duties, of deep and sore inward trials, does not God's Spirit then so bring us into the experience described by the apostle Paul in his epistles [9] to the Corinthians, when we are pressed out of measure, above strength, in order that God Himself might draw nigh, and His presence bring to us all we need?

When the heart is in trouble, it must ascend to the loftiest height, to God Himself. Out of the depths we cry unto Him. The contemplation of doctrines, the remembrance of truth, cannot satisfy us, unless we convert it into present reality, unless we use it as a medium through which we see the countenance of God, as a ladder whereby we ascend to the mountain-height of communion. We need not the atonement merely, but God the Father in Jesus; not redemption, but Jesus Himself our Lord. We then hear again the great unanswerable argument, central and supreme: "He that spared not His own Son, but delivered Him up for us all, how shall He not with Him also freely give us all things?" We do not hear the argument merely, but we behold God. We feel the presence of God, and say, *He*. The believer beholds the loving Father. The soul is now beyond and above mere doctrine. He needs not now to be reminded of the harmony between mercy and truth, grace and justice. The gift of Christ, crucified and exalted, is the true measure of divine love. The eyes of his heart cannot rest on any lower height. The presence of this Christ-giving *God* hushes every murmur, dries every tear, banishes all unbelief. The Father is beheld loving us with the love wherewith He loves the Son. God, who has bestowed on us this greatest gift, never to recall it — who, in order to bestow it, made the inconceivable sacrifice, will freely give us all things with Him. All without Him would be nothing. If God were to give us health and wealth, influence and honour, without and apart from Christ, how miserable we should be! If He were to give us brightness of earthly things, to the obscuring of Christ to our heart, as was the case with Lot and with the Israelites when He sent leanness into their souls, how sad this would be! But whatever God may withhold, and whatever persecutions and troubles He may add, as long as He gives with Christ, He gives "all things."

And what are all things, contrasted with Christ? All things are still finite and exhaustible; Christ is inexhaustible and infinite. All things are outside God; Christ is within God — the only-begotten, eternal, and sovereign Son of the Father. All things are objects of divine favour, according to their position and capacity; Christ, the adequate object of infinite love. "All things" may form helps to bring us to some knowledge of God; they reflect something of His character and glory; they speak some part of the divine message; they encourage and comfort us, to some extent, on our way. But Christ is the perfect, adequate, ultimate revelation of God. In Him dwelleth the fulness of the

Godhead bodily; and He not merely reveals, He imparts; for we dwell in Him, and He in us.

And "all things" are ours; and those of the "all things" God sees we need, are given to us when and as we require them. The same free and self-moving grace which made the stupendous sacrifice, is now providing for our every want, and supplying our every need. Infinite love in the Lord Jesus Christ is constantly flowing towards us; *God is always loving us with the same intensity as when Christ died for us.* Christ's death remains the measure as well as the channel; and all this we are assured of — and why? Because God draws nigh. When we behold Him, this our living God — when we feel the personal presence, then all that is within us asks, "*He* that spared not His own Son, but delivered Him up for us all, how shall He not with Him also freely give us all things?" Then is fulfilled the word of the prophet — "We know that it is *He*." [10]

It is true, without any restriction, that all things are freely given unto us. The mind is not able to take in the immensity of this conception; it is a thought on which the apostle Paul seems to have dwelt often. [11] Let us think, then, of God, to whom all things belong. Before they were created they were His; it was His pleasure. His omnipotence, His sovereignty, that called them into being. How truly are they His! The very possibility of their existence, the very idea of their being and nature, can only be traced to this sovereign and eternal Source. His are all angels and men, all things visible and invisible, things present and things to come. His — and God is from eternity to eternity — Father, Son, and Holy Ghost. All things are of the Father, and all things are in and for the Son, and all things are through the Spirit. God gave all things which were made by the Word unto His Son, the Mediator, the Christ, whom He hath appointed heir of all things. [12] How glorious and rich is Christ! and this Christ is God's gift to us. Christ is ours by the Father's eternal donation, and by the Saviour's own voluntary reception of us, implying His incarnation, death, and resurrection, and His drawing us unto Himself by His Spirit. Marvellous chain! God gives all things unto Christ — God gives Christ unto us; and if Christ is ours, then all things are ours — we are joint-heirs with Him. "He that overcometh shall inherit *all things*."

But how is it that we enter into the consciousness of this amazing possession and boundless wealth? Ah! it is by the old strait gate. We must first become poor. What do I mean by poor— not relatively, but absolutely, poor? Have we given away and renounced everything we had? then we must descend into still lower depths of poverty; we must give up our very self "Ye are not your own." Only when we are not our own, when we are Christ's, are all things ours — "We having nothing, and yet possessing all things." [13] Christ has purchased us with His precious blood, and we are His slaves. Our bodies and our spirits are now God's, both by right of creation and redemption, and, may I add, by our conversion, or by our consent to be absolutely the Lord's. How rich is Christ in the bosom of the Father! how rich are we in the bosom of Christ! How high is Christ at the right hand of God! how high are we, in spirit and reality already, upon Christ's right hand, "the queen in gold of Ophir!"

God draws nigh — and whom shall we fear? Say not, "How are my foes increased! many there be that rise up against me." [14] Say not, My own sins have injured my future; my errors cannot be cancelled; my false choice cannot be rectified. "All things" work together. Marvellous truth! That all things work, we know to our sorrow. The hasty word uttered, the unkind look, the selfish omission — in short, whatever is not of faith and of love — once it goes forth out of the secret chamber of the heart, alas! it works both without and, by a reflex action, it defiles and weakens the soul. The hostile worldly influences, and natural and demoniac powers, all work; but who would have thought they would work *together?* Who could have hoped that the same Lord who hateth iniquity, and whose judgment always begins with His own house, will yet lead the sons of Jacob through the devious and wicked path of their evil, to the love and generosity of their brother Joseph? Here sin is not felt less sinful, but God more glorious. I bow my knees before the God and Father of our Lord Jesus Christ. "How unsearchable are His judgments, and His ways past finding out! Oh the depth of the riches both of the wisdom and knowledge of God!" We thought evil against the Lord; but God meant it unto good. Thus Israel's rejection of the Messiah becomes the occasion of the Gentiles being brought in, and Israel itself shall at length adore the ways of God. Nay, in the presence of Christ we are led still deeper into this mystery, and more unfathomable still is the mystery which explains it. Sin itself has become the occasion of our being exalted into a far higher than Paradise-state. The grace of God doth more abound unto eternal life. One with Jesus, the incarnate Son of God, we cannot regret the fall, though we confess with deep self-abasement our radical and inherited corruption. Sons of Adam are now one with Jesus, the Son of God. Marvellous exaltation of the dust of earth! The eternal purpose and the ultimate object is, that Jesus be exalted. We cannot understand, but we adore, this all-comprehensive and all-victorious counsel of divine love. Satan's victory and man's fall is a dark enigma; but —

"No purpose of wisdom
    Was altered thereby;
'Twas all for the lifting
    Of Jesus on high.
Here Satan was baffled
    In what he had done;
The fall wrought the channel
    Where mercy should run
In streams of salvation
    Which never run dry;
'Twas all for the lifting
    Of Jesus on high."

"We know that all things work together for good to them that love God." It is not merely a devout wish and hope, but a certain conviction. God comforts with realities. The Spirit reveals things freely given to us of God, and then the soul responds, I believe; or, I know; for faith substantiates the unseen. Faith is the most absolute and certain knowledge. Join, oh sorrowful and doubting believers who love God, the great company of thy fellow-sufferers, and say. We know! Hear the apostle Paul. Who ever suffered more? and yet there is no hesitation in his voice.

Experience is not transferable. No human testimony, even inspired, can be to us more than testimony. It cannot be a substitute or a guarantee. But in the experience of the apostle Paul (Rom viii.), every child of God will find both a description of his own, and abundant encouragement, guidance, and consolation.

Here is a man in Christ Jesus. There is now no condemnation to him. Sin has been judged, condemned, and put away. The Spirit of Christ dwells in him. He is not in the flesh; but the flesh is still in him. He has to mortify the deeds of the body; it is a painful and daily struggle Besides, he is in manifold afflictions. He is living in a world of suffering. The very creation even groans by reason of bondage. He also groans within himself, waiting for the redemption of the body.

This justified one, inhabited by the Spirit, is thus saved only in hope. He has still the conflict with sin amid the afflictions of this time, and he has to possess his soul in patience. Thus he draws nigh to God. But there he feels his weakness. His infirmities overwhelm him. He knows not what to pray for as he ought. Full of want, he is silent. But the Spirit of God helps him. He creates within him deep and believing longings after the eternal blessings; too deep for utterance, but not too great for the Father's response. And now he has reached the highest point. He sees *God for us.* God loved us from all eternity, and called us according to His promise. All things must work together for good. Beholding this God as He gave up His own Son, he triumphantly asks: "Shall He not with Him freely give us all things?" Beholding the Lord Jesus who died, yea, rather that is risen again, who is even at the right hand of God, who this very moment in faithful love maketh intercession for us, he asks: "Who can accuse or condemn us? and who can separate us from the love of Christ?" Afflictions and sufferings abound; but in overcoming them, we are more than conquerors; we are not exhausted after the victory, but invigorated, and more deeply rooted in the love of Christ. Perfect is our peace. "Neither death, nor life, nor angels, nor principalities, nor powers, nor things present, nor things to come, nor height, nor depth" — has he forgotten any possible adverse power? is there any other adversary in the realms of space? is there any other shadow of dark and vague apprehension? — "*nor any other creature,* shall be able to separate us from the love of God, which is in Christ Jesus." Love of God in Christ Jesus! It continues sounding in our hearts, as when silver bells have ceased ringing. Love of God in Christ Jesus!

"Is God for me? I fear not,
　　Though all against me rise;
I call on Christ, my Saviour;
　　The host of evil flies;
My Friend, the Head all-glorious.
　　And He, who loves me, God;
What enemy shall harm me,
　　Though coming as a *flood?*
I know it, I believe it,
　　I say it fearlessly —
That God, the best, the highest.
　　Doth heartily love me.
At all times, in all places.
　　He standeth at my side;
What works me woe He hinders;
　　He checks the storm and tide.

"A Rock that stands for ever
　　Is Christ, my Righteousness,
And there I stand unfearing
　　In everlasting bliss;
No earthly thing is needful
　　To this my life from heaven.
And nought of love is worthy
　　Save that which Christ has given -
Christ, all my praise and glory,
　　My light most sweet and fair;
The ship in which He saileth
　　Is scathless everywhere:
In Him I dare be joyful
　　As a hero in the war.
The judgment of the sinner
　　Affrighteth me no more.
"There is no condemnation,
　　There is no pang for me;
The torment and the fire
　　My eyes shall never see;
For me there is no sentence,
　　For me death hath no sting,
Because the Lord who loves me
　　Doth shield me with His wing.
Above my soul's dark waters
　　His Spirit hovers still.
He guards me from all sorrows,
　　From terror and from ill;
In me He works, and blesses
　　The life-seed He has sown,

From Him I learn the 'Abba,'
   That prayer of faith alone.

"And if in lonely places,
   A fearful child, I shrink.
He prays the prayers within me,
   I cannot ask or think —
The deep unspoken language,
   Known only to that love,
Who fathoms the heart's mystery
   From the throne of light above.
His Spirit to my spirit
   Sweet words of comfort saith.
How God the weak one strengthens,
   Who leans on Him in faith;
How He hath built a city
   Of love, and light, and song,
Where the eye at last beholdeth
   What the heart had loved so long.

"And there is my inheritance,
   My kingly palace, home;
The leaf may fall and perish —
   Not less the spring will come;
Like wind and rain of winter.
   Our earthly sighs and tears.
Till the golden summer dawneth
   Of the endless year of years.
The world may pass and perish,
   Thou, God, wilt not remove;
No hatred of all en'mies
   Can part me from thy love;
No hungering nor thirsting.
   No poverty nor care,
No wrath of mighty princes
   Can reach my shelter there.

"No angel, and no brightness,
   No throne, nor power, nor might —
No love, no tribulation,
   No danger, fear, nor flight —
No height, no depth, no creature
   That has been or can be.
Can drive me from thy bosom.
   Can sever me from thee:
My heart in joy upleapeth,
   Grief cannot linger there;

She singeth high in glory
    Amidst the sunshine fair;
The Sun that shines upon me,
    Is Jesus and His love;
The fountain of my singing
    Is deep in heaven above."

[1] Luke xviii. 13, 14.

[2] 2 Cor. v, 19, 20.

[3] Rom. x. 8.

[4] Luke xvi. 25: "But Abraham said" (unto the rich man), "Son, remember that thou in thy lifetime receivedst *thy good things,* and likewise Lazarus evil things."

[5] Compare on the contrast between time life and eternal life. (Chap. xi. 11.)

[6] Compare chap. x.

[7] Genesis xxxii.

[8] Gen. xxxii. 24. This important point, viz., that the conflict is begun by The Man, and not by Jacob, is often overlooked.

[9] In no epistle is the inward life of the apostle Paul so fully described as in the epistles to the Corinthians. Other epistles give us a fuller view of his mental history and his great spiritual experience of grace as distinguished from law. In the epistle to the Philippians we have a more perfect portraiture of his real inmost character, of his deep-rooted joy and peace in Christ. But to the Corinthians he unfolds the conflict, the sorrow, the weakness, the crucifixion, which he constantly experienced. Here we see him in his "weakness," and yet it is a weakness in which he can glory. When we see him weak, we see him strong. "Most gladly therefore will I rather glory in my infirmities, that the power of Christ may rest upon me." In these epistles we may learn what is meant by "the fellowship of Christ's sufferings."

[10] *He* is, according to the Kabbala, one of the names of God, as also "I." Comp. Isaiah and gospel of John *passim.*

[11] Thus in Rom. viii. 28 and 32, all things freely given, and working together. In i Cor. iii. 21, all things are the believer's. In Eph. i. 22, all things put under the feet of Christ at the right hand of God. In Col. i. 16 and 20, all things are said to have been created by Christ, and for Christ, who is before all things (as their eternal Source and beginning. Comp. Prov. viii. and Rev. iii. 14), and by whom all things are reconciled to the Father. Again, in Heb. ii. 8, the apostle emphasizes the "all things" of Psalm viii., that are put in subjection to the Son of Man. (Comp. 1 Cor. xv. 27.) And lastly, the magnificent conclusion of the stupendous argument of Rom. i.-xi.: "For of Him, and through Him, and to Him, are all things: to whom be glory for ever. Amen." We may find in such passages of Scripture all elements of truth and beauty, which have been mingled with dangerous error in Pantheistic systems. Scripture, like Christ, came not to destroy (anything good and true), but to fulfil.

[12] Comp. Rev. iv. 11; John i. 1-3; Heb. i. 2; John iii. 35.

[13] I often remember a little German fairy-tale which used to delight me in my childhood. There was a very poor little orphan girl. She was without home and friends. Alone she went out into the wood as night was coming on. She was very

thinly clad; a single small coin was her only possession, and a piece of bread which she carried in her hand. She met a poor man, and she gave him her piece of money; she met another, and she gave him her bread; she met a little child, cold and shivering, and she gave away her only garment. And now she had nothing — nothing. And she looked up to heaven, and saw the many bright stars, and behold, they all came down in a golden shower, and she was rich and beautiful for ever!

[14] Thus begin the Psalms of poor and afflicted David, after the introductory objective, grand first and second Psalms, with their commencement and end of Blessed. (Ps. i. 1; ii. 12.)

Chapter Nine - Communion with God in Daily Life

"Draw nigh to God, and He will draw nigh to yon" - James iv. 8.

I have endeavoured to lead you into the sanctuary of the hidden life. In speaking of the communion, which divine grace institutes between God and the soul, my object has been not so much to teach or to exhort as to say: Oh, come and taste that the Lord is gracious! — Brethren, there is a river, the streams of which make glad the city of our God. The source of that river is the eternal love which chose us in Christ Jesus, and the end of that river is the everlasting glory; but this very moment the river, full of divine vitality, power, and beauty, flows with fertilising and refreshing power through our hearts and lives. We see it, we rejoice in it; and would it be what it is were its source not in the hidden, mysterious mountain-heights of eternal election? were its end not in the shoreless ocean of infinite blessedness?

As our minds have dwelt on the central experience of communion with God, it may be profitable to consider now the connection between this centre and the large circumference of daily life, with its duties and trials. How is the Sabbath of the heart to be maintained among the alternations of joy and sorrow, activity and recreation? The favourite expression of the day is: Religion in common life. Let us rather ask the question: How can we at all times obey the precept, Draw nigh to God, and enjoy the promise. And God will draw nigh to you? Open your hearts to the love of God, and let all that is within you go forth to meet the Bridegroom. For such is His affection and the tenderness of His heart, that He is not willing to leave you anywhere or at any time without His presence. Let it suffice us to have spent so many hours and days in unnecessary separation from Him, and to have understood so little the attractive power and sweetness of our crucified Lord. *"Love doth the whole —* not part — *desire."*

It is because God is love that it is His desire that we are always to be in communion with Him. Here is our highest privilege, our truest liberty. To follow the Lord fully, to be always giving thanks, and to do all things in the name of Christ, is to walk in the light of God's countenance. It is necessary to think of this, because the world and the worldly mind within us think differently. You know how at all times the world has regarded earnest Christians who endeavour to do all things to God's glory as exaggerated and legal, righteous overmuch, pietistic, Puritanic, and even as hypocritical. How strange that it should not be clear to all that God must be first to those who know and love Him; that Christ, who died for us, claims all our heart and all our life; that the love or fear of God is something so deeply rooted in the heart, that we can never lay it aside or separate it from our feelings and thoughts, our tastes and habits. May we not rather charge those with pietism and hypocrisy who pray to God only occasionally, who reserve the remembrance of Christ and of immortality only for rare and outwardly-striking events of their life? But is it not in accordance with reason, and all the deeper feelings of the human heart, that, having found our one Master and Love, and having entered in by the strait gate on our journey to the pearly gates of the heavenly Jerusalem, we should now wish our life to be of one piece, real, sincere, harmonious, where everything is pervaded by the same spirit, so that whenever our Lord comes, and wherever He finds us, in meditation, or in our daily work, at play with our children, or in social converse, He may find us in loyal and obedient affection? And as this is the desire and aim of the Christian, so is it of the loving God; He has given us both guidance and promise in His word that it may be thus. He has by His Holy Spirit taken up His abode within us; He, according to His promise, will so walk in us, in our thoughts and will, our energies and activities, as well as our feeling and imagination, that, like the apostle, our ways are in Christ Jesus.

Even before the advent of Immanuel — oh, happy Christians who know Jesus! — even before the advent of Immanuel, the saints of God knew that the love of God desired their whole heart and their whole life. Of Enoch it is said, he walked with God. And to Abraham no less comprehensive and loving command was given than this: "Walk before me, and be thou perfect." As a mother delights to be always seeing and watching her child, so all our days are to be spent in the presence of God, and our heart is to seek always to please Him. We are to hide nothing from God; all our thoughts and works, pursuits and enjoyments, are to be transparent before Him; He is to be with us in all our cares and sorrows, in all our prosperity and mirth.

So simple were God's dealings with the patriarchs. But when the law was given through Moses, then, adapting Himself to man's weakness, the Lord minutely analysed and unfolded this *one* precept of walking with God. We Christians are accustomed to regard the law of Moses as *contrasted* with the gospel of Jesus. Ye are not come to mount Sinai, but to mount Zion. By the law is the knowledge of sin, by the gospel the knowledge of salvation. The law pronounces condemnation, the gospel declares eternal life. The law cannot give life, the gospel brings the Holy Ghost. [1]

This contrast is true, and most important. Every Jew who comes to the Lord Jesus experiences this contrast with great distinctness and intensity. So, I suppose, does every one who has gone about to establish his own righteousness. But having experienced this contrast, let us remember that the law is to be considered in another aspect. The apostle Paul does not overlook this second aspect, [2] though he dwells more on the first. In the epistle of James it is always pre-supposed. It is the view which the godly Israelites themselves took of the law while they lived under it; it is the view which, in my opinion, converted and restored .Israel will take, when in a modified and transfigured way, they shall yet fulfil every jot and tittle of that law which was given them for all generations.

David and all the godly Israelites were saved by grace, and justified by faith. They did not seek salvation by the works of the law. Zechariah and Elizabeth, John the Baptist, aged Simeon, and all who waited for the redemption of Israel, rejoiced in grace, and yet walked in all the ordinances of the law. Nay, the apostles themselves, in Jerusalem and among Jewish Christians, observed the law of Moses. And what is this law?

The kernel of the law, given to Israel through Moses, is, love to God and to man. But this general and central principle finds man a member of a family, of society, of a nation. It finds him living in this world of seed-time and harvest, of work and rest, of buying and selling, of sickness and death. What does the law do } The law says, *God loves you;* and God desires that you may have His presence and blessing always. Therefore the law takes cognizance of every branch of human life. It refers to our food and to our garment; it accompanies us from our birth to our grave. It claims our time and our wealth; it connects seed-time and harvest, all natural life, with spiritual truths, redemption-acts, and anticipations of the future glory. There is nothing in our life in which God is not interested, where He is to be absent; there is nothing wherein we may not glorify and obey Him. Israel's whole life is to be a life in communion with Him who chose them, and brought them out of Egypt, the house of bondage.

The law moreover finds us sinful and defiled. Sin is in us and around us. God gave His people Israel laws to remind them of their sins, to bring before them even their unconscious sins, and sins of ignorance, that they may not be like the thoughtless and degraded world, which do not notice or forget their sins, until at last the very power of discerning sin becomes blunted. The inner light itself becomes darkened, and sin, which is no burden on the conscience, is only the more securely enshrined in the heart as an idol. Israel was under the discipline of a law; severe, as it brought their whole life into the light of divine truth and holiness; merciful, in that it provided the assurance of forgiveness and purification. The sacrifices and offerings were ordained that they might continually confess their sin and defilement, and continually receive the consolation of expiation and cleansing. The conscience was purified, and their communion with God continued.

Thus the breadth of the law connected the whole life with God; the depth of the law demanded constant meditation on God's word. The Israelite was to. speak of God and of His wonders to his children morning and evening;

and not merely was the fear of the Lord the fundamental principle of the family, but Israel was taught that our relation to our neighbour was in reality only another aspect of our relation to God. Jehovah identified Himself with the stranger, the widow and orphan, the helpless, the blind; and in doing acts of kindness to them, we are to remember that they are His representatives; hence all commandments concerning them have this seal: I am the Lord.

A godly Israelite would therefore speak in this manner: How dearly God does love us! Our whole life is in His presence. Whether we eat or drink, sow or reap, rejoice in our families or go about our work, in our solitude and in all our dealings with men, we are with Him, doing what He commanded us; pleasing Him, and then receiving His gifts with thanksgiving. True, His law reminds us daily of our trespasses; and not merely of our actual sins, but of our sinfulness and defilement This humbles us; but there is forgiveness with Him. The law reveals to us atonement, and His promise to circumcise and renew our hearts. God makes us constantly draw nigh to Him, and He constantly draws nigh to us. This joyous character of the law, traces of which may still be noticed among the Jews, especially in the spirit in which they observe their festivals, meets us in the books of Moses and the Psalms. Happy art thou, O Israel, is the keynote; blessed are they whom God chooses to approach unto Him.

How easily is this translated into New Testament language, or rather re-translated into the original. For the law was a parenthesis; the gospel was before Moses in the Abrahamic covenant, even as it is from everlasting. The law is now written in our hearts, and the outward and minute regulations are no longer needed. But can the gospel idea of life be less spiritual and comprehensive than that of the law? Is it possible for us to separate eating and drinking, working and resting, family and social life, nature and Providence, from the inward centre of love to God, who redeemed us with the precious blood of Christ? No; the life which we now live in the flesh; mark it, in the flesh; that is, our whole earthly life, in all its aspects, is a life of faith in the Son of God, who loved us, and gave Himself for us. All things must be brought to Christ, and Christ must be brought unto all things. Love doth the whole, not part, desire.

"Love doth the whole, not part, desire.
  My Lord, so doth Thy love require;
    And such is my heart-cry for Thee.
  Thus love by love shall mount yet higher;
    All mine, all Thine, the bond shall be."

                                                              Tersteegen.

The obedience of the Christian, as Leighton observes, though imperfect, hath a certain, if I may so say, imperfect perfection. The whole man is subjected to the whole law, and that constantly and perseveringly. [3]

And now let me suggest a few thoughts, which may encourage and help us. If God loves us, and we love God, if our own will is clinging to His sweet will, then will obedience be an easy yoke and a light burden. Only let us avoid the insipid mediocrity and lukewarmness, which cannot and will not rise to the height of divine love, demanding our whole self— body, soul, and spirit, which never beholds the glory of Jesus, who transforms us by the daily renewing of our mind, even as He changed the water into wine.

I. God Himself Causes Us To Grow In Grace

Who knows human nature as well as He who created it? and who regards our infirmities with such fatherly pity, and bears so patiently with our slow and unbelieving hearts, as the Lord our God? He is our all-wise and all-merciful teacher. The growth and guidance of our spiritual life is altogether in His hands. All things are His; the world around us, and the daily events and circumstances of our earthly life, are under the same government as the spiritual and inward influences of grace in our hearts. The Holy Ghost within teaches, rebukes, comforts, strengthens; and nature and providence are concurrent teachers without. We may often wonder what passages of Scripture we ought to read, and on what subjects of divine truth we ought to ponder. But the page of nature and of providence is opened for us by a higher hand. Let us be docile and childlike, and give our whole mind to the divinely-chosen lesson. Keep your eyes and hearts open. The face of nature, the ordinary events of the day, the remark of a friend, the countenance of a passing child — all are used by the heavenly Teacher to speak to us, and to mould our minds and characters. And as God rules without, so also He alone understands our souls, and governs within. Sunshine and rain, calm and wind, seasons of quiescence and rapid development, work in the inner world, as well as in the outer, under the omniscient and omnipotent direction of divine love. In the spiritual life also we must learn not to be over-anxious, not to please ourselves, and not to substitute human inventions and expedients for heavenly influences. As the Lord said of the lilies, "They toil not, neither do they spin: yet Solomon in all his glory was not arrayed like one of these," so may we say to the Christian who is rooted in Christ, It is for you only to grow, and growth is from *within*. God alone rules in this mysterious sphere; and however thankful we must feel to good teachers and books, we must be carefully on our guard against allowing any one to interfere with our spiritual development. If we abide in Christ, we grow. The ministry of pastors and teachers is divinely appointed, necessary and useful. But there is a morbid desire, not confined to any church, for father confessors, for human direction in the path and conflict of the Christian life. When we feel the need of human sympathy and counsel in our most secret soul-life, have we not the Psalms of David and the Epistles of Paul? Can we ever be lonely with them?

We cannot always sit at the Lord's table receiving impressions of divine truth and favour. The enjoyment of food is only for a short time, while we are eating; in the strength of our daily bread we go on for hours, and fulfil our work. So God gives us, from time to time, the enjoyment of spiritual food; but we are not always to enjoy the fat and marrow; but having obtained renewal of grace and peace, we are to go to our daily work. Glimpses into the higher sanctuary are vouchsafed to cheer and help us on our way. "Often a man in the multitude and pressure of his avocations exercises a more God-pleasing humility and real waiting upon God than in highly-favoured moments of elevated devotion." [4]

We need these seasons of special prayer and meditation, these feasts of communion and joy, these moments when we taste of the powers of the world to come. No Christian life can be sustained without them. The more frequent they are in our lives the better. Such spiritual impressions through the reading" of God's word, in prayer, in the affection and Christian encouragement and hope of a brother, are like refreshing breezes, like the rain and dew, which descend from heaven; they are even more important, they form a capital of strength which stands to us even without our being conscious of it. The Lord's day, the Lord's supper, the prayer meeting, the fellowship with Christ's people, the missionary news, and especially meditation on Scripture, and the experience of the Church as expressed in hymns, are the channels of such influence. Let us highly value them. Young Christians should not have long intervals between meals.

Wait then on God's guidance. Seek to be replenished and refreshed. Be quiet and trustful. "So is the kingdom of God, as if a man should cast seed into the ground; and should sleep, and rise night and day, and the seed should spring and *grow up, he knoweth not how*. For the earth bringeth forth fruit of herself; first the blade, then the ear, after that the full corn in the ear."

II. Alternations of Prosperity and Adversity

God draws nigh in providence. If He gives you prosperity, rejoice and sing psalms; if He sends sorrow, learn again to pray. Let us not merely call a bad harvest, or illness, or loss of wealth, a visitation of God; no doubt God draws nigh in those chastenings; but let us call a good harvest and health and success in our work a visitation of God, to deepen our gratitude, and to encourage us in the ministry of love and in faithful stewardship of His gifts. But all unusual conditions of the mind, joy or grief, are *dangerous,* unless God is sought in them. To be kept in humility, in heavenly-mindedness, and in love to the brethren, when we are prosperous, requires grace; to be patient, trustful, hopeful, in adversity, requires grace. But God's purpose in sending prosperity or sorrow is not fulfilled if we merely avoid their *dangers:* God intends that we should derive *positive benefit* from His dealings. As to affliction, this is more obvious. It yieldeth afterwards the peaceable fruits of righteousness to them that are exercised therein. "Afterwards." For, like the benefits of the Lord's Supper, we may say, the benefits of afiction are not confined to the actual time of our partaking of them. "Afterwards" extends to our whole subsequent life; nay, to eternity.

But God has also great purposes in sending earthly prosperity, providential blessings, family sunshine. He then draws nigh to you. We are commanded to rejoice with them that do rejoice. Hence it is right and pleasing to God to rejoice. Joy ought to be a good, holy, heavenward-drawing thing. Dear friend, when God sends you the desire of your heart and prospers you, may He give you a deep sense of your unworthiness, and a joyous assurance of His fatherly love. Treasure up every impression of gratitude, and every feeling of praise. Let the sunshine call forth abundant thanksgiving. Take deep views of the love of God, whose joy it is to give. Learn to anticipate the cloudless and unspeakable felicity of heaven. Let all the goodness of God lead you to see the beauty of the Lord. As David, after God had given him the wonderful promise, sat down before the Lord in silent thanksgiving and adoration, [5] so look upon all the things which God giveth you richly to enjoy as covenant gifts *with Christ.*

Now it is for you also to give and to bless. Be enlarged in your affections, sympathies, and energies. In the strength of gratitude and love, devise liberal things. Try to serve the Church, and to do good unto all men.

III. Daily Work and Recreation

There is a legend of a monk, to whom in his chamber the Lord vouchsafed to appear in a vision. The vision of Christ brought great peace and joy to his heart. Scarcely had he been thus favoured for a few moments, when the bell was heard, which summoned him to the duty of distributing loaves of bread to the poor. For a moment he hesitated; but he went to his work. Oh, what a sacrifice to leave this glorious vision for the dull routine of duty! But when he returned to his cell, what was his surprise and joy to find the vision of the Lord as before.

It is only sin, not work, which separates us from Christ. To be faithful in little, to be faithful in the perishable things of this world, is a great thing in the eyes of our Lord. It does not matter in what material we work, whether it be mean or costly. "Do all things," saith the apostle to servants, and to us all, "*heartily,* as unto the Lord." The most common and trivial work is to be connected with the deepest. Take an interest in it; do it with all your ability, from the deepest motive, and with the highest aim; do it to please the Lord; He will bless you in the labour, and He will reward you for the work.

Contact with the difficulties and weariness of work, and with the trials of our temper and patience, with the world's injustice or hardness — contact with all this often shows us how weak we still are; how irritable and self-willed; how little inclined to suffer wrong, or to do what is right without being acknowledged and praised; how covetousness, which is idolatry, is not yet uprooted. In all this God holds up a mirror before you, that you may go to the fountain of cleansing. We often fancy that we have reached a high level of Christian character, because we see it clearly and approve of it fervently. Actual life tests us, and teaches us a more truthful, though less pleasing, estimate of our condition.

Glorify God by carrying truthfulness and love, faithfulness and honour, unto all things. We are to *live* the gospel, and to *adorn* it, not merely to preach and to extol it. Men cannot see our hearts, but they can see our good works; and if the works are fruit of the Spirit, they will be *luminous,* pointing to the Father in heaven.

If the love of God or faith is to pervade our whole life, and to enter into all our thoughts and actions, how necessary that itself should be kept strong and pure!

The larger the building is that is be lit up in every part, or to be warmed uniformly, the more you require a strong central source of light and heat. If we therefore speak about religion in common life, as you expand the "common life" you must intensify the "religion." You wish to enrich and enlarge life, your business, your social enjoyments, your knowledge of literature, science and art. I say nothing to discourage or dissuade you; [6] but I appeal to your own common sense when I say. Then you must deepen your knowledge of God and your love to Jesus; you must meditate and pray more frequently; you must increase the motive power. *Keep the heart* with all diligence; keep it pure, unspotted from the world; keep it full; be filled with the Spirit, with love to God and man, with joy and gratitude, with heavenward longings and with God -glorifying aims; keep it strong in ardent love and constant prayer, receiving strength by waiting on the Lord. This is the apostolic exhortation: "Not slothful in business; fervent in spirit; serving the Lord." How forcible is the exhortation of an eminent teacher of the church: "Lo, my brother, if thou wouldst seek out the *still hour,* only a single one every day; and if thou wouldst meditate on the love which called thee into being, which hath overshadowed thee all the days of thy life with blessing, or else by mournful experiences hath admonished and corrected thee, this would be to draw near to thy God. Thus wouldst thou take Him by the hand. Bat whenever in ceaseless dissipation of heart thou goest astray, the sea of the divine blessing shall surround thee on all sides, and yet thy soul shall be athirst. Wilt thou draw near to God? ...Then seek the *still hour.* [7]

Take heed to your recreation. We need recreation. A story is told of the evangelist John. A stranger went to see him, and to his astonishment found him playing with a pet bird. "The bow that is always strung," he said, "loses its strength." But what is recreation, and what is recreation suitable to a Christian? Here no rule can be given, but principles. And even principles are of little use, unless you seek the personal guidance of the Holy Spirit. Only remember to do all things with a clear mind; for whatever is not of faith (though in itself lawful) is sin. Whatever God has forbidden, whatever interferes with our spiritual life and with our daily work, whatever hinders our own growth and our usefulness in the world, let us willingly give up; it would not profit us, or send us back with greater elasticity and vigour to our ordinary path.

Even the wisdom of the world has found out that life would be very pleasant were it not for its pleasures, and that they who most seek pleasure least find it. The search for pleasure and amusement seems to be a characteristic of the present day. A man of deep thought and of a most genial and loving spirit observes: [8] "The present generation is not willing to undertake anything without utilising it for the purpose of pleasure. None is willing to work quietly and contentedly in the sweat of his brow, and without assumption; fetes and holidays are always required. This must use up, more or less, the marrow of life. And how little true enjoyment is in all this! How much suffering, even bitter suffering-, is in what is called life-enjoyment. Truly, one need not *seek* pleasure. If our inward sense is open to pure joy, it meets us everywhere on our path; and we are astonished how people ever came to the thought of purposely seeking pleasure." [9]

The Christian is afraid of everything which disturbs his concentration of purpose and which blunts his spiritual perception and enjoyment. Our great difficulty is, not to lapse into that mediocrity and lukewarmness which in a Christian world characterise the worldly Christian. This danger is always greater in times of peace, when we are without the bracing north wind of persecution; and in times of quiet, when we are without the south wind of special revival. We are then apt to lose the tension and fervour of our first love.

If we wish to use this world as not abusing it, to enjoy all things which God gives us richly, and yet to rejoice supremely and constantly in Him, we must go to the very root of things, and take heed to ourselves. The Scripture gives no minute regulations, but to a sincere Christian sufficient guidance. It may sometimes be duty and true Christian kindness to enter into the social life of those who as yet are not spiritually congenial with you. If we go in the right spirit, and with the true heart, God will help us both to derive no injury and to confer some blessing. We may sometimes be with Christians, the conversation apparently about God's word or kingdom, and yet there may be no real ozone in the atmosphere, no converse of heart with heart, no nourishment, and no refreshment. On the other hand, there may have been no "religious conversation," and yet the animating and restful influence of affection, friendship, and the contact of minds living in the fear and light of God.

This is a large subject, and yet one on which each one must find for himself what is right, safe, and profitable. Only let us be sincere, and avoid all Pharisaism. The next best thing to grace is nature. Only let us be heavenly-minded, and avoid worldliness. For the time is shortened; the coming of the Lord, blessed be God, draweth nigh: "it remaineth, that both they that have wives be as though they had none; and they that weep, as though they wept not; and they that rejoice, as though they rejoiced not; and they that buy, as though they possessed not; and they that use this world, as not abusing it; for the fashion of this world passeth away."

It is narrated of Diogenes, that when Alexander the Great asked him to request a favour, the only thing that poor man wished of the conqueror of the world was, not to stand between him and the sun, whose genial light and warmth he was enjoying. If Diogenes stands for the Christian, Alexander for the world, and the sun for Him who is the light and joy of His people, we may look upon this story as an allegory: all that the Christian really wishes is, that the world should not obstruct and intercept the rays of happiness which come to him from the heavenly sanctuary.

If we are anxious always to look *first* to God, and to place Him between us and our circumstances, and the people we have to deal with, then we shall be able to exercise love and patience, and to be calm and peaceful at all times. We have to deal with God on the one hand, and with our fellow-men and circumstances on the other. Now the great point is, how we place ourselves. If we allow people and circumstances to come between us and God, then the smallest provocation, disappointment, and difficulty may obstruct to us the light of heaven, and intercept the supply of grace and strength. But if we place God between us and the men we have to deal with, and the work we have to do, we shall walk in light and in love; for God is light and love, a translucent and strengthening medium. Look first at Him, and then at men and things. Have you met with trial? do not look first at the trial, and then at God, with the question: Does God, who allows this sorrow, love me? Look first at God, and with the renewed assurance of God's love, look at the trial, and say, God chastens whom He loves. When the servant, to whom his master had forgiven a great debt, met his fellow-servant who owed him money, he forgot the mercy he had experienced; but if the kind and merciful countenance of his benefactor had stood before him, between him and his debtor, could he have acted with such severity and cruelty? If we looked at all men through the medium of Christ crucified, we should possess that love which in all things endureth and hopeth; we should treat all with patience and meekness. If we looked through Christ our strength at all duties and trials, we should be able to say, "I can do all things through Christ which strengtheneth me." When Shimei cursed David, David remembered that it was God who permitted this trial. Before his feelings settled on Shimei, they rested on God, and humbled themselves before Him. Place then Christ as the medium of light and love and strength between you and all men and all things. Remember, God's will is our sanctification. "We are opposing God's method of working if our life has a tendency to incapacitate us for the enjoyment of prayer at *all times.* If by needless excess of worldly cares— if by inordinate desires, which render it impossible for us to accomplish our objects in life *without* such excess of care — if by frivolous habits — if by the reading of infidel or effeminate literature — if by an indolent life — if by any self-indulgence in physical regimen — we render the habit of fragmentary prayer impracticable or unnatural to us, *we are crossing the methods of God's working.* Something has gone wrong, *is* going wrong, in the life of that Christian who finds himself thus estranged from filial freedom with God." [10]

Start daily and often with the joy of God's salvation, and end always with the praise of God. Begin with the gospel, the glad tidings of God's love in Christ. Say to yourself. He first loved me. I have obtained mercy. God has given me Christ. Let your heart be first established by grace. Rejoice in the Lord. Do not think of giving unto God until you have received from Him. And let no sense of your unworthiness prevent your taking hold of the boundless and all-sufficient grace of God. A sense of divine *love* will keep you more humble, more loving, more active and fervent in service than anything else. This is the only starting-point of Christian life — the assurance of God's love through faith in Christ. And therefore, to those who have not yet come to God through Christ, the only practical message is, Repent and believe. You cannot carry religion into daily life till you first have it in your heart; and you cannot have it in your heart till you come to Jesus the Saviour. Starting with the joy of God's salvation, let our end always be praise. Thanks be to God for His unspeakable gift. Blessed be God, who hath called us unto immortality and glory. Faithful is He who hath called us, who also will perform it. As with thanksgiving we are to make our requests known unto God, so thanksgiving is to be the prevailing and the ultimate note of our life. At last all our thoughts and petitions will end in praise. For God will perfect that which concerneth us. [11] We shall yet more than ever praise Him, and only praise Him. "Awake, psaltery and harp: I myself will awake early." After I have remembered all His benefits and promises, I will forget even them in the contemplation of Himself, and say to my soul: "Bless the Lord; my soul doth magnify the Lord, and my spirit hath rejoiced in God my Saviour."

See, every veil is removed. There is the veil of *Moses;* for Israel could not behold steadfastly the face of Moses for the glory of his countenance. There is also the veil upon the heart which has turned from God in unbelief. There is the veil of creaturely distance, for the seraphim veil their faces before the glory of Christ, the great Jehovah. But *we* all, who by the Holy Ghost through Jesus draw nigh, we *all,* weak and strong, babes in Christ as well as experienced soldiers who endure hardness, and fathers who have known Him, that is from the beginning, we all with open face behold the glory of the Lord, we see the glory of God, the image of the Invisible, the beauty of the Lord; in the mirror of the gospel we see Immanuel, Christ, who is God above all, and yet our Brother. Thus beholding, thus adoring, are we changed into the same image from glory to glory, even as by the Spirit of the Lord. [12]

"Draw nigh to God, and He will draw nigh to you."

[1] Heb. xii. 18; Rom. iii. 20; Gal. iii. 5.
[2] Gal. iv.
[3] That this threefold perfection of obedience is not a picture drawn by fancy is evident in David (Ps. cxix.), when he subjects himself to the whole law, his feet (*v.* 105), his mouth (*v.* 13), his heart (*v.* 11), the whole tenor of his life

(*v.* 24). He subjects himself to the whole law (*v.* 6), and he professes his constancy therein (*vv.* 16, 33), "I shall keep it to the end." — Leighton.

[4] Bengel.

[5] I Chronicles xvii. 16.

[6] In an essay on "Poetry and Christianity," Harless points out clearly, that poetry which refers to "worldly things" is not necessarily poetry of the unholy and ungodly spirit of the world. He recommends Christians to study and to enjoy thankfully the gifts of the poet, and quotes the words of an earnest theologian of the pietistic school: "They who are always busy with sacred subjects get at last accustomed to them, and none are in greater danger of hypocrisy than ministers;" or we may add, what are usually termed decided Christians. A pious man need not be narrow, as, alas! the narrow man is not always pious.

[7] Tholuck.

[8] Rothe, *Ethik*.

[9] The following remarks on social life are translated from a sermon (on John iv.) of Schleiermacher, whom none can accuse of narrowness of views or sympathies. They seem to me as important and wide in their application as they are beautiful: "How much of our time do we devote to social intercourse of various kinds. There are not many among us who confine themselves to such a small circle of closely-united men, among whom no special occasion and reason is needed to speak also about the highest interests of life, but who consider them as a topic of conversation; but in those larger circles, to which we all belong, more or less, in which there is neither the intimacy of friendship, nor the entire strangeness which subsisted between the Lord and the woman of Samaria, how much and how long do we dwell on trifles, on isolated and unimportant occurrences! and when we touch on personal matters, which concern not merely the absent, how rarely is it done in such a way that a salutary train of thoughts is called forth, and that the heart is influenced, to connect the unimportant with what is truly great! How rarely does anything permanently good result from those social meetings, even when they achieve their design of cheering our earthly path, and dissipating the anxieties of life! I do not require that graceful cheerfulness, and exhilarating play of thought and conversation should be banished, and that we should always endeavour to look into the secrets of the heart, and to speak of eternal and divine things. No; but can and ought there to be a moment in the Christian's mind, in which it is not his desire to contribute to the inner life of those with whom he meets even in this larger circle — to contribute to it out of that life which dwells in him in glorious and vigorous fulness? And this desire, which is the mark of true Christian love, ought it not to run as a golden thread even through our harmless relaxation and mirth, and be able to find the suitable and favourable moment, as our Saviour did, to lead our social conversation from trifles unto the great subject? We leave an innocent and pleasant circle, and feel more animated and cheerful; but this feeling

may be true or not. If there has been nothing truly important and great, the conversation which has amused and interested us by its brilliancy and humour, leaves nothing behind to strengthen us when we return to the cares, the duties, and the fatiguing troubles of life. But if such social intercourse has given us a deeper feeling or more correct understanding of some truth of eternal importance, if it has afforded us a new insight into some department of the spiritual life, or gladdened us by the discovery of beautiful and noble aspirations of some kindred soul who is interested in the same great purpose, then we carry away an enriched feeling of life into the hours of labour and toil. There is stirred within us a high energy, which brings to us protracted blessing. Something out of the stream of living water has flowed into our soul, and we are strengthened for the next moments of anxiety and work.
[10] Phelps.
[11] Psalm cxxxviii. 8.
[12] 2 Cor. iii. 15-18.

Chapter Ten - The Indwelling of God By Love and By The Holy Ghost

I. Union With Christ (Unio Mystica).

The teaching of Scripture on the union of Christ and believers belongs to the highest and most precious disclosures of revelation. It is, as it were, the most holy place of the sanctuary. All manifestations of divine grace prepare our minds and hearts for the reception of this mystery. Before the advent it was symbolised and promised that God will dwell in us, and we in Him. Israel, as a nation, failed in realizing the high idea of God's love; but as Israel's failure became more evident the promise of the Messiah became more distinct; of the servant of God, in whom the Spirit dwells in sevenfold plenitude, and through whom there would be at last granted unto Israel the presence and glory of Jehovah among them, and the indwelling of the Holy Ghost in their renewed hearts.

Yet this was in the future, though many godly and specially-favoured Israelites had a deep and strong realization of present communion with God, and wonderful anticipations of a still closer union. For such expressions as "The Lord is my light and salvation," "The Lord is our refuge and strength," "The Lord our righteousness," are evidently the language of an experience high above that which only knows that God gives protection and strength, that He sends light into our hearts, and clothes us with righteousness. How much must these men have known of the mysterious indwelling of God in us, to which all our good thoughts and works are to be traced, and of our indwelling in God, who alone is our salvation! And what further prophetic insight was given them of the still brighter and yet nearer approach of God in the promised One may be inferred from such passages as the forty-fifth Psalm, which speaks of the marriage of Him who is fairer than the sons of men, and into whose lips grace is poured, with Israel, the bride, who stands at His right hand in gold of Ophir. Yet is this royal Bridegroom spoken of as God, whose throne is for ever and ever. This psalm is the bud, out of which has flowered forth the song of songs. The Beloved who is here spoken of is none other than God incarnate. In no other book of Scripture, except in the book of Revelation entrusted to the disciple whom Jesus loved, have we a description of the beauty, grace, and strength of the Son of God in His perfect humanity. The Spirit who was in holy men of old testified within them of the glory of Jehovah, the heavenly Bridegroom.

Let us not forget, however, that before the day of Pentecost Israel, even including John the Baptist, did not see the "mystery" of the Church as it is now revealed. The union of Christ and the Church is the mystery of our dispensation, prepared in the gospels, and especially in that of John, who dwells so fully on the promise of the Holy Ghost and the indwelling of the Father and the Son by the Spirit in our hearts, but fully announced in the epistle of Paul to the Ephesians. While it was given to the apostle of the Gentiles in harmony with the peculiar character of his conversion and mission to unfold this mystery, it was the object of the Joannean epistle to dwell on the spiritual and ethical aspects of the New Testament Church.

The Scripture in teaching, or rather making known and unveiling mysteries, leads us to heights which are far beyond our vision, and yet it does not dazzle our eyes with light, which only confuses; nor does it puff up our minds with speculative knowledge, which leaves the heart cold and the daily life untouched. Clearly and definitely is this supernatural union with Christ taught, and yet we exclaim, Great is the mystery! And as there is no vagueness, though the well is deep, so is there no cold and barren abstraction. The apostle connects with this mystery the most lowly exhortations, such as lie not one to another, for you are members of the one body; such as the warning against impurity, for our members are the members of Christ. Here are also the sweetest consolation and brightest hopes of the Christian. The Head is in glory, and will He leave us behind? The last Adam, who loved the Church and gave Himself for it, loves and cherishes us as His own body, and after our earthly discipline will present us to Himself a glorious church, not having spot, or wrinkle, or any such thing.

Illustrations from every sphere are used to describe to us the reality and the vital character of this union. As the building rests on the sure foundation, so the Church is built on the Rock. Believers are lively stones, who by faith are resting on Christ, and in whom God has His habitation through the Spirit. As the vine gives vitality and fruit-bearing strength to the branches, so Christ is the indwelling life, and the resurrection -power of all who are grafted into Him. As Eve, or the woman, is beloved and cherished by Adam, out of whom she was originally taken, so that they twain are one flesh, so is the Church, sprung into life on the resurrection morn, beloved by Him; she is one Spirit with the Lord. Of her it is said: "We are members of His body, of His flesh, and of His bones." Still higher goes the Scripture; for we are taught that Christ is the Head, and that we are the members; that we are one; that the Church is His body, the fulness of Him that filleth all in all.

If to these illustrations, than which nothing can be more distinct and definite, we add other declarations of the word of God, that we have become partakers of the divine nature, that we are the righteousness of God in Christ, that Christ is in us; to use his own solemn words, "As thou, Father, art in Me, and I in thee," we may well exclaim, "Such knowledge is too wonderful for me; it is high, I cannot attain unto it."

It is evident that two dangerous aberrations are possible. The mysterious depth of these words of Scripture may tempt some to reduce them to a lower and more intelligible and comprehensible meaning. Accordingly we may think that all the union spoken of is that of affection and gratitude, of love and trust, of congeniality and obedience. [1] It is quite true that without these elements there can be no union between God and us, between Christ and the church; but it is also true that these very features of our union must lead us to the knowledge of a deeper union out of which they flow. For whence this affection? It is not of nature, but shed abroad by the Holy Ghost. Faith also is the gift of God, and by it Christ dwells in the heart. And of obedience or fruit, we know that only the abiding in the true vine can originate or sustain it. Our union with Christ is therefore not merely ethical, but real (physical). Christ is really the source and continued strength of our life. If Christ's union with the Father were merely a moral one, then similarly is ours with Christ. But Jesus saith, "As the living Father hath sent me, and I live by the Father: so he that eateth me, even he shall live by me." Spiritual conformity to Christ and continued obedience to His holy and sweet will are most precious features and results of that real and hidden union between Christ and the believer, of which God the Father is the author, in which Christ is the centre, and the Holy Ghost is the connecting link. The word. Baptism and the Lord's Supper, are channels, faith the receptive organ.

The root of this union is the eternal counsel of Godhead; the realisation is in the incarnation, death, and resurrection of the Son of God. The ingrafting of the branches, the formation of the members, the betrothal of the bride, is the work of the co-equal Spirit; the consummation, the marriage feast of the Lamb. Of which mystery neither the church nor the individual believer must ever abate one jot or tittle. The mystery of the incarnation has changed every thing upon earth, giving us more than an angel's nature, since God became man. He who is perfect God became perfect man, and now (mystery of mysteries) has taken our manhood into God, made it one with Himself, never to be parted from Him, not lost, as in the ocean of His divinity, but for ever glorified, filled, in-oned with God. "Nearer and closer than any union, with a nearness inferior only to that oneness of the divine nature, is the oneness of our nature with that of God in the person of our ever-blessed Redeemer. Above angels and principalities and powers, is this our human nature glorified in God, with that glory which the Son had before the world was." And we, who believe, are one with Jesus. We cannot comprehend this mystery, and we do not measure it by our feelings; we hold it fast by faith, and if we were unbelieving or silent, the Lord's supper would declare it — Christ and the Church are one; Christ by His death has become the life of His people.

But while we seek to avoid the danger of lowering the meaning of the Scripture statements, we may err in another direction. We may lose ourselves in vague and indefinite notions, and thus lose the real power and consolation of this truth. Let us bear in mind that the marriage of the Lamb has not come yet; and, what is closely connected with this, that many aspects of this truth refer only partially to the individual believer, they refer to the whole company and organism of the elect. There is therefore much which at present we cannot realize; for we do not as yet possess it; and it is difficult for us even to form a conception of that union between Christ and the saints which shall finally be manifested and consummated.

There are two aspects of this truth, which are, strictly speaking, experimental and practical. The one is, that the indwelling of God is His love shed abroad in our hearts; the other, that Christ dwells in us by the Spirit. The two aspects are substantially the same; but it may help us to consider them separately. Is the love of God in me? Have I the Spirit of Christ?

II. God Is Love

Love appears lovely to all. There is no word which possesses an attraction so strong and sweet as love. When we say that God is love, and that love is the fulfilment of the law, and that love is greater than faith and hope, the assent of all is immediately gained. Why is this? There is a problem here which leads us into great depths. If love is so lovely, man is without excuse; for the law demands nothing but love — "Thou shalt love the Lord thy God with all thy heart, and all thy soul, and all thy strength, and thy neighbour as thyself;" why have we broken it? The gospel announces nothing but love; why do we not accept it?

Men who have no knowledge of sin, and of the salvation which divine love has secured, have very confused and erroneous thoughts when they say, God is love; and yet we are glad that the word love has such a powerful attraction; for we say unto them: The love which you ignorantly exalt we declare unto you. "Herein is love, not that we loved God, but that He loved us, and sent His Son to be the propitiation for our sins." This love of God is not merely revealed to us, but by the Holy Ghost it is shed abroad in our hearts. And this perfect love of God now dwelleth in us. It has kindled love in us, as light is begotten of light; but it is not our limited and weak love to God which gives us confidence, which casts out all fear, which begets hope, that maketh not ashamed, and which is the constraining power of our life; it is *God's love to us* which dwells in us — the infinite and eternal love of the Father through the self-sacrifice of the Son, revealed and imparted by the co-equal Spirit.

None know the love of God, except those who know the God of love. The whole Old Testament may be considered as the exposition of the word God; the whole New Testament as the unfolding of the word love. If we say, "God is love," do we know what is meant by God? He is light, and in Him is no darkness at all. His majesty and truth, His righteousness and justice, His mercy and compassion. His condescension in electing a people, and His jealousy for their exclusive loyalty and allegiance, all the features of the divine countenance, must be seen in union, before we pronounce with the spirit and the understanding that mysterious word "God." As is the idea of God, so will be the conception of love. Can we call that love, which can tolerate evil — evil, which is the opposite of love, and destruction of it? Can love be indifferent to the true blessedness of its object, or can love be satisfied without response and return? The love which the world attributes to God is unworthy of the name. According to this view, God remains unknown and unloved, and instead of holiness, power, truth, grace, harmoniously blended, bringing the beloved object into an atmosphere of peace, and communion, and conformity with God, there is but a feeble indulgence and pity, which overlooks sin, and leaves man in his wretched condition, without the assurance of divine favour, and without a renewal of his heart.

Such is the usual undefined and unproductive feeling concerning divine love. But take the Old Testament revelation of God, and you are prepared to understand the New Testament declaration — God is love.

God is good, and the fountain of good, and of good only. He must needs hate iniquity, as that which is opposed to Him and to all blessedness. He chooses men that they may be brought near unto Himself. He therefore teaches them by the law to know His character, and to know their sinfulness. By the bitter conviction of sin and guilt He turns them from sin and destruction; and by the sweet revelation of His grace and favour He draws them unto Himself. They now understand that He loves them, and that He hates their sin; *they* are to live, *sin* is to be destroyed. Their true self He seeks, and therefore He is jealous; an undivided heart and an unconditional surrender of the will is His demand, and that because He is loving. Yet it is not sufficient that Jehovah — "I, even I," — forgives and removes His people's sin, giving unto them His righteousness, He even gives them a new heart, and puts His Holy Spirit within them, so that they are now able to love and serve Him. Nay, He has promised to dwell in them, and to walk in them; so that He who loved them, who redeemed them, is also He who lives in them, who by His Holy Spirit renews and sanctifies them with a most real, intimate, and mysterious union and communion with Himself. This is the substance of the Old Testament revelation. Jehovah condescending in election, redeeming in righteousness-grace, renewing and indwelling by the Spirit, — who is a God like unto Him?

This God is *Love;* so the New Testament still further unfolds. Love seeks the object itself; God seeks us, our true self. Shall I say our immortal spirit? No; God seeks us — man according to the divine idea — body, soul, and spirit; His desire and purpose is to possess us, knowing, loving, serving Him, and rejoicing in Him as our fountain and centre. Love rescues us, by the stupendous sacrifice of Christ, delivering us from the condemnation of sin, from the curse of the law, from the power of death, and from the thraldom of Satan, and separating us, by a painful and yet blessed co-crucifixion, from sin, the great opposite of love. Love then communicates itself to us, and that by the Holy Ghost, so that we see, accept, and respond to the Father's election and the Saviour's redemption by a will divinely wrought in us — the first act of liberty, the birth-moment of the emancipated new man. Love then takes up its abode in us.

This most real experience is described in various ways. When God reveals and gives unto us His love in Christ Jesus the new life commences. Contrasting it with our past condition, we call this crisis "regeneration." Regarding the change that is effected in our will, we call it "conversion" or turning unto God. Looking at the attitude in which the soul then stands to the divine love, we call it "faith." But viewing it as the starting-point of a new course, it is the receiving of the Holy Ghost as an indwelling spirit, it is the entrance of Christ into the heart, it is the communication of that *love of God* which is perfect, infinite, unchanging. God now dwelleth in us because we love, and because He hath given to us of His Spirit. Thus are we betrothed unto Christ and sealed by the Spirit; but the purpose of love is not yet fulfilled, for the marriage of the Lamb is not yet come. We wait for the adoption; that is, the redemption of the body. When we shall see Jesus as He is, and be like Him, when, delivered from the body of sin and death, as the children of the resurrection, changed into the likeness of the transfigured Saviour, we shall know as we are known; and in perfect union and communion with the Head and all the saints shall evermore serve Him in childlike humility, in brotherly like-mindedness, with the undivided and restful affection of the wife, and with the mysterious and at present incomprehensible unity of incorporated members; then, brethren and companions in tribulation and in the kingdom and patience of Jesus Christ, then shall we know that God is love, then the words of Jesus shall be fulfilled, "I in them, and thou in me; that the love wherewith thou hast loved me may be in them, and I in them." [2]

When the sinner returns to God, he finds himself surrounded by divine love. As a newborn child, he opens his eyes on a world of love. Now he understands the shepherd-love of Jesus, who sought and saved him, who laid down His life to bring him unto God. Now he understands the motherly love of the Spirit, who, by the enlightening and searching power of the Word, rescued him out of the darkness when he lay helpless, and brought him a precious jewel into the treasury of heaven. Now he understands the generous and joyous love of the Father, who adorns him with Christ as his robe and righteousness, giving him the ring of adoption and inheritance, instead of the fetters of sin and fear, endowing him with the power of the new obedience, so that the heart being enlarged, he is able to run in the way of God's commandments. They begin to make merry and to be glad, and the feast lasts throughout time and eternity. [3] Love compasses us about. The past appears to us as an island, enclosed by the ocean of love — love electing, love dying, love drawing. The future appears as the endless manifestation of love and enjoyment of it. In the present we see love above; God is for us; love around us; Jesus is with us; love within; the Spirit of Christ is given us, assuring us of the love of God, and constraining us by the love of Jesus.

Jesus has the pre-eminence. He is the way of divine love to us. Only in Him could redemption come to us, including deliverance from evil, and restoration unto glory; only in Him can we behold, accept, and return the love of God to us. Jesus has the pre-eminence, yet, in order that we may come to Him, whose Son and gift He is; we confess Christ to be the Lord, to the glory of the Father. And as Jesus points to the Father, so He reveals and gives Himself unto us by the Spirit.

And thus are we brought again to the ultimate mystery, God is love, because God is Father, Son, and Holy Ghost. He is love, from everlasting to everlasting. Creation is the result, but not the beginning of love. Redemption is the manifestation of God as love, and therefore points to a love of absolute necessity and eternity. God is love, not God became love. Above all creation, above every beginning and end, from everlasting to everlasting in Himself, God is love; Father, Son, and Holy Ghost is the one living and loving Jehovah. It is into this love that we are planted by the incarnation, death, and resurrection of Jesus. "The Father loveth the Son." "I and my Father are one." Here is the ultimate foundation of our salvation and glory.

But when such thoughts of the eternal covenant and the future glory are too high for us, there is a centre where we find repose; there is a magnet which draws our hearts; there is one point where the eternities meet, and all mysteries become irradiated with the sweet light of peace. It is the little hill outside Jerusalem; it is the cross outside the camp; it is Jesus crucified for us.

"Time's undefined dimensions,
  Eternity's expansions,
    Can give my heart no rest;
  When on such depths I ponder,
  My soul is lost in wonder,
    And feels with awe opprest.

"The Son of God is dying.
  Faith hears the Saviour crying,
    'Tis finished! Lamb of God,
  I see now my election,
  And glorious resurrection.
    In Thy most precious blood."

III. If We Love, God Dwelleth In Us

We cannot love God until we believe that God loves us; but as love presupposes faith, so there can be no faith in God's love without our loving Him. We are saved by faith only; but faith is never alone. It contains the germ of love.

As Scripture teaches, that there is no love except by faith in God's love, so Scripture equally teaches that there is no faith without love. We know that God loved us, because Christ died for us; we know that having thus loved us while we were enemies, He loves us much more now, being reconciled to Him by the death of His Son. The love of God is now in our hearts, and it is thus that God dwells in us. The apostle John, in harmony with all Scripture, gives us two descriptions or tests of the indwelling of God. [4] The first is love; the second is the possession of the Spirit.

"If we love one another," he says, "God dwelleth in us." [5] It is narrated that the aged apostle was carried into the assembly of the saints, and that the only words he addressed to them were, "Children, love one another." It seemed to him the comprehensive summary, the highest point Christian experience can reach. If God is love, then, wherever He is, there must be the presence, the power, the blessing of love. If God is in us, then, wherever we are, there must be love, going forth as light, consolation, help; forgiving, restoring, healing. But why does he not say: If we love *God*, He dwelleth in us? Why is his exhortation, "Love one another"? Because he is anxious we should not deceive ourselves. We may imagine we love God, when we only love His gifts, or His worship, or the enjoyment of His promises, and of our contemplation of His truth. To love God is to love Love. If we, then, do not live in an atmosphere of love, we do not live in God. If affection and tenderness, and the spirit of helpfulness and kindness, do not animate us towards the brethren whom we see, do we possess the loving mind towards God, whom we do not see?

The apostle John was called by the ancient Church the theologian. He was compared to the eagle, who soars high above mountains, and gazes into the bright sun. It was given unto him to testify of the glory of the only-begotten. And yet although in the writings of the beloved disciple we are instructed in the deepest mysteries, we find there also the simplest and most practical aspect of truth. He who lived in the contemplation of God, and whose fellowship was with the Father and the Son, beheld most clearly that reality of love which is the source and strength of all obedience.

The first epistle of John dwells chiefly on love, viewed in its comprehensive character as love to God and man. Here we must not separate what God hath joined together. Our Lord was delighted with the answer of the scribe who had recognized love to be the sum and substance of the law; and Jesus has taught us that the second commandment, though necessarily second, as it rests on and is born of the first, is yet equal to the first. The beloved disciple emphasizes love to our brethren. He presents it as the evidence of regeneration, of our having passed from death unto life; and not merely as the evidence and symptom of our condition, but as the condition itself. He that loveth his brother abideth in the light. God is light, because God is love. If we walk in love, we walk in God and in light.

If we examine our own hearts, we shall find the truth of John's teaching. We do not need to soar up into high and mysterious regions, or to wait for influences of a special nature, if we wish to enjoy fellowship with God. If we look into our hearts, and if we find there clouds of darkness, envy, jealousy, apathy, uncharitableness, if there is a lack of sympathy and brotherly kindness, or if we cherish unforgiving thoughts, if we withhold sympathy and help from our brother, these clouds are not merely between us and our fellow-man, but between us and God. Let them be dispersed, and you will see within you the reflection of the bright, peaceful blue of God's heaven. God dwelleth in you.

If we regarded the indwelling of God in this light, we should be more truly humbled and more truly comforted. Many, it is to be feared, walk without the power and enjoyment of God's light, because they exercise themselves in things too high for them; and this does not *humble* the soul, although it perplexes it. Whether I love my neighbour, and walk in lowliness, kindness, tenderness, imitating the example of the Lord, and illustrating the apostle's description of love (I Cor. xiii.), is a question requiring for its solution no metaphysical and theological subtlety, but leading to much real humility and to a deep sense of our selfishness, pride, and hardness of heart. To whom then can we go but to the Lord Himself, who is love; to Jesus, who died for us, to deliver us from our selfish hearts, that we may live unto Him?

Love to God cannot exist without love to man. It is incompatible, as need not be pointed out, with hatred, even the hidden beginnings of it, as anger in the heart, envy and malice. It is also incompatible with indifference; for how can love to God manifest itself and find room for activity except in relation to our fellow-men? And it is the very nature of love to manifest itself and to work.

All we know of God in Christ and by the Spirit immediately involves in it love to man.

God is Father, and from this simplest truth the Lord Jesus deduces the command, "Love your enemies," be filled with love, springing out of the spontaneous and inexhaustible fulness of the Father's love; love all, and not merely those who by their love deserve and attract yours. (Matt. v. 44.) God is Father, in a more special sense, of all who are born again, and by faith have received the adoption; and again the immediate inference is, "Whosoever believeth that Jesus is the Christ is born of God: and every one that loveth Him that begat loveth him also that is begotten of Him."

If we look to Jesus, we see in Him an embodiment of the two commandments in their unity. He loved God, and therefore laid down His life for the sheep; He loved man, and therefore He sanctified Himself for us. Loving Him, we love the Father and we love mankind, and especially the church. One with

Christ, we are members one of another; and the more we understand and feel the love of Christ, the more we enter into the great purpose and final reward of the Saviour, the *Church,* which is His body, the fulness of Him that filleth all in all. This is the new commandment which the Lord gave His disciples, that they love one another. It is new, because the love of God in the incarnation, and the self-sacrifice of the Son of God, and in the gift of the Holy Ghost as an indwelling Spirit, was new, although testified and foreshadowed in the law and prophets. It is the one commandment, because in keeping it we enter into the meaning as well as the fruition of the highest manifestation of God in Christ, of the new covenant of the blood of Jesus and the Holy Ghost.

If we love the Lord Jesus, we have been transplanted out of the world into that element and community of which Jesus is the centre. We belong now to the flock, to the brotherhood, to the body, in which all members are organically united, growing together, and strengthening one another. In every Christian we behold some feature of Christ's countenance reflected, some gift of grace which we do not possess, some manifestation of the Spirit in which we are deficient, and thus we learn *Christ* in him, and our faith and love are stirred up and increased by that which he supplieth, In and through him we learn to love Jesus more fully and with deeper insight. And the very defects, failures, and sins of our brethren give us occasion to exercise ourselves in the love of Christ, which in all things shows faith and endurance and hopefulness. We learn to *wash the disciples' feet* by our prayer and kindness; by our counsel and example we endeavour to deliver them from the defilement of sin and the infirmities and inconsistencies of their walk.

As we cannot love the Father and the Lord Jesus Christ without loving man, so the indwelling of the Holy Ghost brings before us still further the essential necessity of love in its comprehensive meaning. He is pre-eminently the Spirit of communicating and sanctifying love. To be in the Spirit is to love; to walk in the spirit of adoption, in the Spirit of the Son, is to walk in love, *as Christ also hath loved us*, and given Himself for us unto God an offering and a sacrifice for a sweet-smelling savour. The Holy Ghost is the real [objective] bond between Christ and the believer, between the believer and the whole Church. How then can the Spirit be in us unless we love the Head and the members? If as individuals and as congregations we desire to be more conscious of the presence of God's Spirit, and to be strengthened with might by His Spirit in the inner man, let us begin with *love to one another;* for the Spirit is preeminently love. The connection between brotherly love and the manifested blessing and power of the Holy Ghost is brought before us in that beautiful and touching Psalm: "Behold, how good and how pleasant it is for brethren to dwell together in unity! It is like the precious ointment upon the head, that ran down upon the beard, even Aaron's beard: that went down to the skirts of his garments; as the dew of Hermon, and as the dew that descended upon the mountains of Zion: for there the Lord commanded the blessing, even life for evermore."

IV. The Indwelling Spirit

The gift of the Holy Ghost as the indwelling Spirit is the consummation of all divine promises, and the crown and fruit of the Saviour's death and resurrection. Jesus has not left us orphans, but He has, according to His promise, sent His Spirit, and so dwells in us, and we in Him. Because the Spirit dwells in us, we can say, "To me to live is Christ." We pray in the Holy Ghost; the very fainting of our hearts and longings of our souls in unutterable groanings are the Spirit's breathings; any good words we utter, it is the Spirit of our Father which speaketh in us; our diligence and zeal arise only out of the energy which worketh in us mightily; our whole spiritual life is continually sustained and nourished, enlightened and directed by the Holy Ghost, in whom the Father and the Son have taken up their abode within us.

Sin is now not merely against God above us, and against God for us, but against God within us. It is against the very presence of Him who in amazing love hath taken up His abode within us. It is against the very presence of Him who proceedeth from the Father and from the Son, *through that humanity in which He died for our sins,* and is now glorified as our Lord, our righteousness, and life.

And if we ask, What is the manifestation of the Spirit? what is His first gift? what the first and most important fruit of His indwelling? the answer can only be. Love. Nay, the indwelling of the Spirit is the indwelling of love. The love of God is shed abroad in our hearts by the Holy Ghost, who is given unto us. It is for this reason that the epistle of John coordinates these two aspects of the indwelling of God in us; the first, that we love, and the second, that we have received the Spirit.

Love is the substance of the law, and instead of the law, we have now received the Spirit; for the law could not give life, and the Holy Ghost can only come through the preaching of the gospel. Hence the indwelling of the Spirit must be love, or the fulfilling of the law. (Compare Jer. xxxi. and Gal.)

Love is the new commandment of Christ. If we love, we abide in Him. But the Spirit is the real, vital link between the Vine and the branches. Hence the Spirit is love. Love is the very being of God. The Father loveth the Son, His co-equal and co-eternal Son, by the Spirit, who is the love and bond of both; "He loveth the human nature of His Son as joined in one person with the Son of His love; and now He loveth us as joined on to Him, whom He loveth everlastingly. And that we may love Him, He hath given us His Spirit, that Spirit of love in whom the everlasting Father loved His co-eternal Son, so that He, who is the bond of both, should be the bond of our love with the Father, and with one another." Our nature is now exalted at the right hand of God, and the fulness of the Godhead dwelleth in Jesus bodily. And through Jesus God has given us His Holy Spirit to dwell in us, that thus in truth and reality we might be made partakers of the divine nature.

As the Spirit is sent of the Father, so He comes from Christ in His glorified humanity. It is to assure us of this most important and precious fact that Jesus, after His resurrection, breathed upon the disciples, and said, "Receive ye the Holy Ghost." God breathed into Adam, and thus Adam was a living soul; from Christ, the quickening Spirit, from His inmost body, proceed the rivers of living water, even the Spirit, now dwelling in us. Hence the advent of the Spirit is the fruit of Christ's return to glory after He had finished His work of atonement. The Spirit is the pledge as well as the bond of our indissoluble union with the incarnate Son of God.

Now God is no longer to us outside ourselves, but within. The Spirit of God is the Spirit of our spirit. Our whole inner life is under His omnipotent and all-tender influence. We ascend to God by the Spirit. God communes with us by Him. How solemn is the exhortation, "Grieve not the Holy Spirit." We were once without the indwelling Spirit, and then the law of God and the gospel of Christ were outside of us, external authority and invitation; and the warning was, Obey, yield. But now Christ dwells in us by the Spirit. It is Jesus Himself who is represented by the Spirit in us. Grieve not the Holy Spirit; for He, like Jesus and the Father, is no mere influence or power, but the Holy One, living and loving, who is pained by the resistance and disobedience of men. It is written of Israel, that God sent unto them the Messenger, in whom was His name; "that He was afflicted in all their afflictions; that the angel of His presence saved them; that He bare them, and carried them all the days of old. But they rebelled, and vexed His Holy Spirit." [6] Behold the fulfilment. Christ is our great Captain and all-loving, merciful, and compassionate Immanuel. We are guided by Him, and upheld by His sympathy and intercession, during our journey in the wilderness. The Holy Ghost is given unto us; He is God, light and love; grieve Him not.

As in every sin against Jesus men dishonoured and rejected the Father, so in every sorrow we cause the Holy Ghost we grieve Jesus, from whom He comes — Jesus, who by Him dwells within us. And who is it that will gladden us if we grieve the Spirit, the only giver of consolation and joy? He is the oil of gladness, which, from Jesus the High Priest and Head, descends on all the members of the mystical body.

[1] "Many have explained the words Abide in Christ, and that Christ abides in us, to mean simply our having thoughts about Christ. Thus, when they meditated on Christ's sufferings and death, they said Christ was in them, and they in Him; there are still many among ourselves who think that Christ is in them, because they remember Christ and what He endured, they do not esteem faith in Christ to be the true spiritual being of Christ in them and our being in Christ; but dream that there is eternal life in their running, thinking, and fancying about Christ, and busying themselves with semblances, which was much the practice under the Papacy, and is still, that meditating on Christ's sufferings is considered to be the indwelling of Christ in the heart, whereby Christ's sufferings are misunderstood and subverted. But the Lord does not say, Your thoughts of me are in me, or my

thoughts are in you; but I, I am in you. He does not speak of bare thoughts, but that I, with body, soul, godliness, righteousness, with sins, folly, and wisdom, am in Him, and that Christ, with His wisdom, righteousness, holiness, and blessedness, is in me." — *Luther*.

[2] Rom. viii. 23; Phil. iii. 20, 21; Eph. iv. 13; John xvii. 23 to end.

[3] Luke xv.

[4] I John iv. *passim*.

[5] Simple words of the "Würtemberger Original" Flattich: "Because God loved the world and delights in human beings, I would like to take more delight and pleasure in the humblest person than in the most beautiful buildings and possessions. I am therefore glad to have so many people about me, and that I can exercise myself in love, and have pleasure in men; and I notice that if I have a feeling of displeasure even towards one individual, it mars my happiness; but when I can love all, I am happy."

[6] Isaiah lxiii., to which the apostle Paul evidently refers in Eph. iv. 30.

Chapter Eleven - With Jesus, Now And For Ever

[1]

A celebrated German mystic used to write in the albums of his friends this motto:

HE, TO WHOM TIME
IS AS ETERNITY,
AND. ETERNITY
AS TIME,
IS DELIVERED
FROM ALL STRIFE. [2]

The experience of every Christian testifies of this truth. The Lord, who is from everlasting to everlasting, is the dwelling-place, the safe and peaceful home, of His saints in all generations. Even now God is our portion, and the eternal life is begun. Our life is hid with Christ in God. We are strangers and pilgrims on earth; our citizenship is in heaven, and we are the inhabitants of an abiding city. It is equally true that we are strangers and pilgrims *in time,* and that we are living the eternal life. We can more easily realize the local contrast, earth and heaven, than the contrast, time and eternity. Yet the life of faith is the life which breathes the atmosphere of eternity, which looks on the things unseen and eternal, and beholds the glory of God. And as the heavenly citizenship is ours while we are still walking on earth, so the eternal life is ours though we are still in time. In the most transitory and earthly things, such as eating and drinking, we are to keep in view the eternal ocean, the glory of God. In the midst of cares and sorrows, toil and labour, conflict and struggle, we have a still deeper and more real possession, even that hidden life in which there is no pause and no change, but perennial sunshine and inexhaustible fulness, perfect rest and the peace which passeth understanding. Part of the daily bread which our heavenly Father gives to His children on earth is to enter daily into the secret place of the most high, and to be in eternity. [3] Eternity is wrought into time. He who lives in eternity finds time and strength for every good work which God lays before him. [4]

But not merely is time as eternity, but eternity is as time. We look forward to another age. We await the Lord's return and the Father's house, in which are many mansions. It is this same Jesus who loved us and redeemed us, who is now dwelling in our hearts by faith, who will come again and receive us to Himself, that we may thus be for ever with the Lord. It doth not yet appear what we shall be, but it is no vague, shadowy, and colourless infinity to which we look forward. Even now we know and love God; we have union and communion with Jesus, the Son of the Father; we have fellowship with the brethren; we praise and serve, nay, we rejoice with joy unspeakable and full of glory. Even at present we are come to mount Zion and the heavenly Jerusalem, and the angels of God worship by ministering unto us the heirs of salvation. [5] When the Lord returns, the hidden life and the hidden glory will become manifest. Without imperfection and sin, without conflict and danger, delivered from all bondage and sorrow, we shall be with Jesus and the saints in perfect love, and in the joy of perfect service. Eternity is to us as time, the age to come, the continuation, the manifestation, and perfection of our present and true existence.

It is the Lord Jesus who gives this eternal life; in Him only can we find rest. How soon in our earthly existence do we become conscious that we are not at rest! We remember childhood. "The young spirit has awakened out of eternity, and knows not what we mean by time. As yet, time is no fast-hurrying stream, but a sportful, sunlit ocean." [6] But how soon do we leave this mysterious morning-land of our earthly life, and discover that we are imprisoned in darkness and in sin! It is man's misery which bespeaks his grandeur lost. It is because he is a dethroned king that he feels unhappy without the royal spirit, dignity, and power. It is because he is fallen — he who was created in God's image— that he feels hampered and fettered when he sees himself the creature of time, surrounded with things that perish, and unable to find anywhere that "type of perfect in his mind." If we had no idea of eternity, could we have the idea of time, and feel the sadness and bondage of it? If there is no fountain of living water, whence and why our thirst? If there is no heaven, no eternity, who has invented the language of the human heart, the deep sigh, though all the waters of this life have been tasted?

And in this darkness and misery we are conscious that sin is the deep and bitter root, and that not without a great and painful wrench (may we not call it death?) can we come to the true human life. Meanwhile we go on existing; but it is not life; for there is no present in it. It is made up of remembrance of the past, and anticipation of the future. Memory and hope meet, and the meeting-point is called the present. But this so-called present is empty; it is not filled with anything substantial and satisfactory. We seek diversion; that is, we flee from the emptiness of the present. It is instructive to study the testimony of the poets of all ages and nations on this point. [7] They all confess, that apart from God there are only broken cisterns, which can hold no water. We never are, but expect and dream we shall be blessed. This life without a true present is in reality death. What the world calls enjoying life is enjoying death; living in pleasure, men are dead while they live. [8] Worse than pain and care, more exhausting than suffering and anxiety, is this empty and dreary existence, in which the soul has no bread, no water, no sunshine, no love; in which the immortal and God-breathed spirit knows only time-life. [9]

But, blessed be God, Jesus has come! The life was manifested, and we have seen it, even that eternal life which was with the Father. [10] He has come to give rest unto the weary and heavy-laden, light to the mind, peace to the conscience, love to the heart, and all is real, divine, eternal, inexhaustible. Not as the world giveth, for the world does not give freely; it only lends to recall, it only exchanges and barters, often taking more and better things from us than it bestows. The world's gifts are not what they seem to be. They do not enrich the heart; they do not last; and, above all, they are dead things which cannot give life. But Jesus gives, and gives Himself. Himself is the light, the life, the peace. God and man, eternal and in time, sinless and a Saviour, the Holy One and Redeemer; there is no question, no longing, no disease, which He does not solve, fulfil, heal. He is the way, where before we saw no way, no possibility of either departure out of our misery, or arrival in the far-off eternal city. Only by Him can we come to the fountain of living water, to the Father.

And as we anticipated, though dimly, it is by a great and painful wrench, something like death. He says, "You must be born again." Mysterious words! He is to be our life. We are near Him; but this is not enough, we must be transplanted, as it were, grafted into Him. And He can draw us into Him only by His death. The new birth can only be by our looking unto Jesus lifted up as the Sinbearer, [11] In this look there is the wrench, the death. By the cross of Christ we have been crucified to the world, and the world to us; the old man has received his death wound, and we have begun to die daily. But it is also the birth, the commencement of the resurrection-life.

And now we live! We have a present. Not merely has the past lost all bitterness — for our sins are forgiven, blotted out, and forgotten — and the future possesses no terror, but the present is full of life and reality. For the Lord is our God. When we think of Him, when we love and serve Him, when we pray and hear His voice, we do not merely exist, we *live*. "To me to live is Christ." We are *with* Jesus. And in this present we possess all the treasures of the past and of the future. Now we know that He, who loved us with an everlasting love, has taught and guided us from our youth, and that He has prepared for us an everlasting home of blessedness.

The remembrance of the first advent, culminating in the sacrifice of love on Golgotha, and the hope of the Lord's return, bringing glory and joy to His ransomed Bride; this past and this future form the element in which the Christian lives; they are, so to speak, blended in his consciousness, and form his true present, his real, blessed, eternal life. The Lord's Supper is the emblem of the inner and hidden life. Li the midst of all the fleeting and distracting things of time, the constant change and fluctuation of things temporal, there is quiet fruition, perfect repose; it is at the table of the Lord, it is in communion' with Him who is the life. Here is the most vivid remembrance and realization of the death of Christ; here is the most vivid anticipation of the return of the Bridegroom. It is the Spirit of God who makes both the first advent a present and constant reality to the Christian, and who influences and animates us by the hope of the second coming of our great God and Saviour. Without the teaching and power of the Holy Ghost, we do not realize or possess in the present either the death or the glorious return of our Lord. To the Christian, Christ's death and resurrection are a present fact, power, consolation, an ever-new separation from sin and birth unto holiness —painful to the flesh, yet full of peace and joy to the Spirit. "I feel as if Jesus had died only yesterday," said Luther.

"I can see Him even now,
 With His pierced thorn-clad brow,
 Agonizing on the tree:
 Oh, what love! and all for me,"

sings another saint. "Dear dying Lamb" is the invocation of another, when contemplating redeeming love. And the return of Christ is that ultimate and yet most proximate point to which the believer constantly looks, towards which is all his hope, and from which he receives constantly the deepest impulses and motives for purification and diligent labour. "This Jesus" is our all. "This Jesus," born in Bethlehem, crucified on Calvary, risen and ascended — behold, our Past — "shall so come again" — behold, our Future. The same Jesus and Saviour shall return unto us, coming meekly as the Prince of Peace, and in the fulness of love. The grace of God, bringing salvation, hath appeared — this is our sunrise — teaching us to wait for the appearing of our great God and Saviour — this is our perfect, never-ending day. If through the faith of the first advent we are enriched by Christ in all utterance and in all knowledge, so that we come behind in no gift, then truly we are waiting for the coming of our Lord Jesus Christ, we go forth to meet the Bridegroom.

II. It is a blessed persuasion, wrought in us by the Spirit, that nothing shall be able to separate us from the love of God, which is in Christ Jesus; not death, and what is still more, not "life" (Rom. viii. 38), with its duties and trials, and our constant failures and sins. It is difficult to believe that in all our departures from God, and in all our sins, the ever-watchful and tender eyes of divine love and pity never depart from us; and that the Saviour, who will never allow any of His sheep to perish, is ready to heal and to restore, and to give us even through our falls a fuller knowledge of his all-sufficient grace. Nay, grace never ceases her work within our hearts; the Holy Spirit, though grieved, is ever abiding in the soul. And as this is the constant source of our failures and falls — that we forget that we are with Jesus, and instead of leaning on Him as our only strength, gird ourselves, and go whither we choose, so is this our deepest and sweetest repentance — to return to the Lord, who never leaves us, and to find Him the same loving Saviour, ready to receive, us and to draw us close to Himself. [12]

Often we think we are far from Jesus; we have no sense of His nearness, and it seems to be night. Yet all the time we are with Him. Our life is far deeper than our consciousness — I sleep, but my heart waketh [13] — and when we complain that we cannot discern any progress or growth, we are with Jesus, and His grace is training and moulding us in infinite wisdom. There are divine delays; the soul mourns over the lack of wine, and the Master seems only to rebuke us; but we are with Jesus, and He will soon manifest His glory, and gladden us with His love. There are monotonous and irksome duties, lowly and commonplace occupations, and the spirit knows not at first that to be faithful in this appointed and humble path is the true and royal dignity of God's children. But we learn that here also we are with Jesus; and we remember the thirty years of His quiet and obscure life at Nazareth. He did not preach or show any miracle; yet neither in heaven nor earth was ought so lovely in the Father's sight, or so God-glorifying, as He who was called the carpenter's son.

There are manifold temptations. Who can enumerate or even classify them? Luther's division is a simple one — temptations which are painful, and temptations which are pleasing. When we experience trouble and disappointment, ingratitude and reproach; when our will is crossed, and our cherished expectations frustrated; when we are prevented from carrying out good and favourite projects, we are tempted to impatience, doubt, bitterness, despondency. Or when we have prosperity, health, the praise of men, and other things pleasant to the natural man, we are tempted to pride and subtle self-conceit, to lukewarmness in prayer, and hardness of heart. There are sudden temptations, fierce and vehement, when the enemy storms the citadel of the soul by an unexpected and violent attack. There are gently insinuating temptations, when the tempter approaches us like a serpent. When it is given us to remember that we are always with Jesus, then we betake ourselves at once to Him, and He gives us wisdom and strength. This is Satan's masterpiece, to beguile us from the simplicity which is in Christ Jesus. As a child says, "I do not know; I must ask my father. I cannot go; I must ask leave of my father;" so let us always retreat into Christ. He is always near, and within sight of the subtle fowler's snare, and the roaring lion, we are "safe in the arms of Jesus."

We are with Jesus in our daily life. He is Alpha; we have no other starting-point. Because He loved us, we love Him; because He saved us, we now live to serve Him. He is the beginning and strength of all our outgoings Godwards. We forget this so often. We admit that apart from Christ we cannot think a good thought, say one good word, and do one good act; but do we always pray, as really believing, that we thus depend on Christ? And after prayer do we continue in this dependent attitude and trustful expectation? We practically think we can live, and walk, and do the daily life-path work without this constant drawing on Christ, or we fancy we must continue in sin and weakness. When we remember we are with Jesus, when we behold the blessed Master, full of love and power, willing to be unto us mouth and wisdom, guide and strength, then it is easy to pray without ceasing, and to be of good courage, to go on and prosper. Our daily trespasses do not then discourage us, and fill us with the disappointment of a wounded vanity; but we return immediately, and with deep humility, to the Lord; for we are not astonished at the discovery of our vileness, and are willing to abase ourselves before God, and to trust in His mercy.

And if Jesus is Alpha, so is He Omega. We pray in His name, we live in His name, and we desire the glory of His name. To whom should ascend our thanksgivings but to Him who gave us all, who wrought all things in us? Who is the end, but He who is the beginning? To whom and for whom are we to live and to work, but to Him who redeemed us, the author and finisher of faith? Let us then do all things unto the Lord. To please Him, and to be approved of Him, is the only right aim. Thus remembering continually the "tribunal of Christ," we shall do all things heartily, and then Jesus Himself is our immediate reward, and we can look forward that we shall not be ashamed before Him at His coming. [14] Love makes obedience sweet. The presence of Jesus, our divine Lord, will make our lives not only solemn, but also strong and vigorous. It will quicken and sustain every energy. He is with us who loves us with more than a father's affection, more than a mother's tenderness, more than a brother's sympathy, more than a friend's faithfulness, more than a bridegroom's delight. This thought will animate us. We need never be lonely and faint. In all the meditations of our hearts, in our intercourse with men, in our silent and secret sorrows and struggles, in our public words and actions, we are with Jesus. His presence is our rest and strength.

In this communion with Jesus we are conformed to His image. We learn to possess the mind, which was in Him. "O Jesus," exclaims an aged servant of the Lord, "let thy whole walk on earth stand before my eye, that I may be continually renewed thereby, and that I may be a savour of life, filled with the fruits of righteousness, to them with whom I live, and for whom I pray!" "Thy whole walk on earth." It is summed up in one word — love. It is symbolized by one symbol — Lamb. Here we see love to God and man perfectly united, constantly blended. Here we see One, who was always meek and lowly in heart, who came to minister and lay down His life. Every thing in Christ's earthly life breathes the spirit of the Son and the spirit of the Servant. He came in lowliness, and yet He showed forth His glory. Every gospel incident, and every saying of Jesus, is of everlasting importance, and possesses inexhaustible vitality. The Holy Spirit brings before our soul Jesus, as He was on earth, as a present living reality; Immanuel, God with us, in our joys and sorrows, in our daily walk and struggle.

The character of the Lord Jesus, as described by the evangelists, surpasses in depth, beauty, and comprehensiveness all that human thought and imagination could ever reach. It unites perfectly and harmoniously elements which are blended nowhere else. His innocence, purity, meekness, and gentleness co-exist with His burning zeal, unremitting vigour, uncompromising severity, and holy indignation. His love of solitude and His sublime loneliness never prevent Him from entering into the wants and sorrows of men, or from descending to their ignorance, doubt, and weakness. His teaching, so divine and yet so human, is perfectly lucid and clear, direct and convincing; in the simple intuition of His filial spirit He speaks the words of eternal life, in which all is truth, transparent, all-sided, eternal. He is a man of sorrows, and acquainted with grief, and yet He never produces the impression of austerity and moroseness. He rejoices in spirit; He changes water into wine at the marriage feast of Cana; He takes little children into His arms and blesses them; He defends the joy of His disciples because the Bridegroom was with them. We feel in His presence, as in the presence of the Son of God, holy, solemn, peaceful; of one who possesses without measure the spirit of joy and gladness, of joy unspeakable and full of glory, of joy which the world cannot understand or take from Him, which even in the prospect of the bitter agony of the cross and the darkness of death is so strong and sure of itself, that He can comfort His disciples, and bequeath to them as His legacy, "that they might have my joy fulfilled in themselves."

Jesus, the Son of God and Son of man, must needs be above our comprehension; the union of the divine and human surpasses all our thought. And yet is this "man Christ Jesus," who is above all — God blessed for ever — the most distinct, living, and bright reality to us, divine, infinite Light, Love and Life wrought into true and real humanity! And the Spirit of God keeps this wonderful and attractive Image before our eyes. Jesus is our model, and from the nature of the case our only, one Master. Jesus is heavenly-minded; as He Himself expresses, the Son of man who came from heaven *is* in heaven. In Him we see that to be spiritually-minded is life and peace. But in this stranger and pilgrim on earth there is nothing morbid or ascetic; His spirituality is so deep and free, continuous and joyous, strong and full, that there is no effort, no unevenness, no disturbance of His affectionate and humble and helpful intercourse with those around Him. His obedience to the Father, His fulfilment of the divine law, is perfect. In every detail of life, in every word He utters, in every feature and attitude. He is in the presence and conscious enjoyment of the Father, always glorifying and manifesting Him. And yet there is nothing in Him that savours of the spirit of bondage; He walks with the step of royal liberty. His life is full of light and rhythm. [15]

He loves God and man; He loves His disciples with a special love and tenderness, yet rebuking and disciplining with holy severity. He loves mankind, especially the poor and helpless, the sorrowful and contrite. His object is always to heal and to do good; He is the Light of the world; He came to bless and to save. Whatever man's attitude may be, He cannot deny Himself. He is perfect Love.

We are to be followers of Christ, continuing His testimony of truth, and His ministry of love. Sent by Him, as He was of the Father, we are to show forth Christ in our characters and lives. Let us then be with Jesus, as an example and model. It is only when we know the saving power of His death and resurrection that we can be followers of Jesus We need the Pentecostal light of the epistles to gain a spiritual and practical understanding of the gospels; for the exalted and glorified Redeemer leads His children to walk in the footsteps He left behind. When we walk on this narrow but luminous path, we are with Jesus.

The Spirit brings us to Jesus, the Royal High Priest *in heaven;* and He also brings us into fellowship with the *earthly* life and obedience of our Saviour. "As He is, so are we in this world;" [16] behold, this is our great task, and our true dignity.

III. *We are with Jesus, and therefore separated from the world.* We know there is a false separateness from the world by eccentricity, in ambition, in pride, in Pharisaic conceit, in self-centred isolation. But the words of our Saviour, "They are not of the world, even as I am not of the world," have so impressed us with their awful solemnity and wondrous love, that we look with suspicion and dread on everything that tends to weaken their force, and to make us forget that cross of our Lord Jesus Christ, in which alone we are to glory. Remembering that our citizenship is in heaven, we are sure that they over whom the apostle Paul wept were not opposed to the *doctrine* of the cross, but they were enemies of the cross of Christ itself. They did not believe in the crucified Saviour with the heart, with the will; they minded earthly things. The expression is earthly, not sinful; the contrast is between this present time-world and the heavenly eternity.

Men make little of sin, and they doubt or deny the existence of Satan; and in like manner they also deny the "present evil world" to be opposed to the Spirit of Christ. But we know these are our three great enemies, and we must think of no compromise, of no armistice in our warfare against them.

The simple fact that we know Jesus separates us from the world; for "the world seeth me no more." It is Christ's peace which now fills our heart; and if our joy is to be full, it must be because Christ's joy is in us. The love of the Father cannot be in us if we love the world, and the things that are in the world. Our treasure is in heaven, and our heart waiteth in expectation of the Lord, and of the heavenly inheritance.

We do not forget that God loved the world which He created, that the earth is the Lord's, and the fulness thereof; we do not forget that God's saints have always rejoiced in the manifold works of their Father, and adored the wisdom and power of the Creator. We are taught that not merely things future are ours, but also things present; that to those who are not high-minded, but trust in the living God, God giveth richly all things to enjoy. We remember that we are called to admire and think on everything that is honourable and lovely, to take a cordial interest in the whole sphere of human affection and friendship, intellect and energy.

But yet we are strangers and pilgrims on earth. We know that whosoever drinketh of the water which this world giveth shall thirst again. We can never forget the transitory nature and subordinate importance of all earthly joys and gifts. We cannot possess, we cannot desire, that satisfied happiness and absorption in the present things, even though they be sinless, which worldly men either have or seek. We can see no blessedness in being rich, or strong, or great, in being anything in this world. By the cross of Christ we have been crucified to the world, and the world to us. And this great separation was actually effected in us when our heart was renewed, when our will was broken, when the Spirit drew us to *Jesus*.

How can we ever in this earthly life be free from this feeling of sorrow, of longing, when we are with Jesus, of whom it is written, "A man of sorrows, and acquainted with grief"?

> "A pilgrim through this lonely world
>   The blessed Saviour passed;
> A mourner all His life was He,
>   A dying Lamb at last.

> "That tender heart that felt for all,
>   For all its life-blood gave;
> It found on earth no resting-place,
>   Save only in the grave."

Are we identified with Him? Are we at all like Him? Then we cannot be what the world calls happy. The Lord pronounces them blessed that mourn.

But as we are delivered from the tumultuous and eager striving after happiness in the present life, so we have now in God that peace which passeth all understanding, which the world can neither give nor take away. We have within us the well of water springing up into eternal life. Instead of seeking them, we regard the pleasures and recreations of life not without misgiving; for we feel they are apt to cloud our peace, and to blunt our enjoyment of the heavenly blessings. The world seeks diversion; we seek to collect all the energies of our souls, and concentrate them on the great object of our heart's desire. The world seeks to go out into wide and boundless fields; we desire to abide within, where Jesus sups with us, and we with Him.

If it is objected that such a character is melancholy, the answer is, And what if it is? Is not Paul's description of the Christian "*sorrowful,* yet always rejoicing"? [17] But what if it be only thus that we can have the true joy of the Lord? If only thus, dead with Christ, the light and power of the resurrection-life gladdens our heart? If only by this constant inward dying and fasting, by this constant self-restraint in earthly prosperity and joy, by this constant prayer and humiliation of the Father spirit within while the sons and daughters are feasting, [18] we can abide in the presence of Him who alone can make us lie down in green pastures, who anoints the head with oil, so that our cup runneth over? What if only in this way we can draw what is truly good and precious out of the present life?

How can we ever forget this truth, when it is declared on every page of Scripture, and to be read in every feature of Christ's countenance and walk on earth? And what truth has been more frequently and emphatically asserted of the Saviour? Why did He put the cross so prominently and almost deterrently before those who professed themselves willing to follow Him? Five times He utters the axiom of the eternal life, the essential mark of the heavenly-minded.

1. "He that findeth his life shall lose it: and he that loseth his life for my sake shall find it." [19]

2. "For whosoever will save his life shall lose it: and whosoever will lose his life for my sake shall find it." [20]

3. "For whosoever will save his life shall lose it; but whosoever shall lose his life for my sake and the gospel's, the same shall save it." [21]

4. "Whosoever shall seek to save his life shall lose it; and whosoever shall lose his life shall preserve it." [22]

5. "He that loveth his life shall lose It; and he that hateth his life in this world shall keep it unto life eternal." [23]

It is evident from the variety of expressions used (and they are all full of meaning) that this was a leading, favourite, and oft-repeated thought of our Lord.

"Two loves," said Augustine, "have made two cities: the love of self, reaching on to the contempt of God, has made the city of the world; the love of God, reaching on to the contempt of self, has made the heavenly city."

"Something every heart is loving —
    If not Jesus, none can rest;
  Lord, to Thee my heart is given,
    Take it, for it loves Thee best.

"*Thus I cast the world behind me,*
    Jesus mast beloved shall be;
  Beauteous more than all things beauteous,
    He alone is joy to me."

IV. *We are with Jesus;* and yet, when we are most truly with Jesus, and feel His presence and our oneness with Him, there arise also most vividly the thought and *hope of His return,* when the heavenly Bridegroom and His Church shall meet to part no more, when we shall be for ever with the Lord. Spiritual communion with Jesus, even when most precious and sweet, as in the Lord's Supper, never can so satisfy the heart as to exclude the desire of His return; nay, it is part of the feast, that it contains the promise, "till He come." The Spirit is our comforter during the absence of our Lord; He is not a substitute for or instead of Christ, but by the Spirit we are joined to the Lord, and Christ dwells in our heart. But the Spirit Himself says in us, "Come, Lord Jesus." Let us then cling to those simplest and sweetest words of the Lord, "I will come again." The hearts of the disciples were full of sadness; the thought of ever having to part with their beloved Master had never been realized by them, and the whole world seemed dark and lonely in the prospect of His leaving them. Jesus comforted them. And this is the comfort, that in His Father's house there are many mansions, that He is going to prepare a place for them, and that He would come again and receive them to Himself. As if He said unto them, "This world is not your home; you are indeed strangers here below. My Father's house is the home of those who through me are the Father's children. I leave you for a little, and during this little while my love is with you, and my heart and hands working for you: I go to prepare a place for you. And I myself will come again, never to leave you, but to receive you to myself for evermore." It is as when a mother says to her children, "I'll soon be back again." Who can misunderstand the words? Spiritually He is never absent; He is always with His people: His peace. His love, His grace. His power — when have they ever left His children? But we have not at present His personal, actual, bodily presence; we do not see Him. Christ our life shall appear, and then we shall be made manifest with Him in glory. Thus the promise of Jesus was confirmed by angels to the disciples, who gazed with wonder into the heavens; and all apostolic teaching directs our hearts to the return of our Lord.

They who are with Jesus yet desire to depart and be with Christ, which is far better. They are at rest, and have found in Jesus their peaceful and eternal home; and yet are they home-sick; for while they are in the body they are absent from the Lord. Even when Jesus is nearest, when He brings them into the banqueting-house, their hearts are gladdened by the thought — Till He come! They are waiting for the revelation of Jesus Christ, although in all things they are enriched by Him, in whom all blessings of the covenant are theirs. Waiting is the attitude, the incessant heart and life-work of the Christian. It is the heart that waiteth. It is there that the flame must be nourished with the sacred oil, the flame which only the eye of God discerns; it is there, where Jesus is Alpha and Omega, the root and strength, as well as the end and object, of all our life. The true waiting for the Lord, and going forth to meet the Bridegroom, is hidden from outward observation. It consists in our earnest endeavour to please the Lord, to be accepted of Him." In consists in our keeping ourselves in the love of God, while we look for the mercy of our Lord Jesus Christ unto eternal life; in our abiding in the True Vine, and thus bringing forth the true fruit, which only the heavenly gardener sees, and of which He only eats. It consists in guarding anxiously the door of the heart, that out of the multitude of influences seeking entrance there, none may be admitted which would be displeasing to Him to whom we belong, and who claims our undivided love.

We believe that our ascended Royal High Priest is preparing for each believer, for each child of God, a peculiar and individual place. As one human countenance differs from another, as the glory of one star differeth from that of another, so there is a great variety and manifold peculiarity among the children of God. Each has a name, known only to the Lord and himself, and the Good Shepherd, who knows each sheep by name, is preparing for each "a place." All are children and heirs, all are united in the Father's house; but each finds as he was led personally during the time of his earthly pilgrimage, so the end of the way is also personally adapted to him. Thus all our earthly experiences have an eternal result. As our spiritual life progresses on earth, our eternal mansion progresses. Jesus fits us for our future abode, and prepares our future abode for us. "Let not your heart be troubled;" infinite wisdom and love is preparing an inheritance for you, and preparing you for an inheritance. But let the heart awake; let us be faithful unto death, that we may obtain the crown of life. We are with Jesus. He is all — the beginning and the ending. With Him all our hopes begin, in Him all our hopes are crowned. Only by Him are we children, and therefore heirs: only grace can lead to glory. The end is most inseparably connected with the beginning; for this is the beginning: He loved us, and washed us from our sins in His own blood. This is the beginning: A poor lost sinner beholds the Lamb of God. And this is the end: To see and adore the Lamb. In the Father's house we shall be for ever with Him "who was dead, and is alive for evermore." "I have a desire to depart and to be with Christ."

Thank God that towards eternity
   Another step is won!
Oh, longing turns my heart to Thee
   As time flows slowly on!
Thou Fountain whence my life is born,
Whence those rich streams of grace are drawn
   That through my being run.

I count the hours, the days, the years,
   That stretch in tedious line.
Until, O Life, that hour appears
   When at Thy touch divine
Whate'er is mortal now in me
Shall be consumed for aye in Thee,
   And deathless life be mine.

So glows Thy love within this frame,
   That, touched with keenest fire,
My whole soul kindles in the flame

   Of one intense desire,
To be in Thee, and Thou in me.
And e'en while yet on earth to be
   Still pressing closer, nigher!

Oh, that I soon might Thee behold,
   I count the moments o'er!
Ah! come, ere yet my heart grows cold,
   And cannot call Thee more!
Come in Thy glory; for Thy Bride
Hath girt her for the holy-tide,
   And waiteth at the door.

And since Thy Spirit sheds abroad
   The oil of grace in me,
And Thou art inly near me. Lord,
   And I am lost in Thee,
So shines in me the living Light,
And steadfast burns my lamp, and bright,
   To greet Thee joyously.

Come! is the voice then of Thy Bride;
   She loudly prays Thee come!
With faithful heart she long hath cried.
   Come quickly, Jesus, come!
Come, O my Bridegroom, Lamb of God!
Thou knowest I am Thine, my Lord;
   Come down and take me home!

Yet be the hour that none can tell
   Left wholly to Thy choice;
Although I know Thou lov'st it well.
   That I with heart and voice
Should bid Thee come, and from this day
Care but to meet Thee on Thy way,
   And at Thy sight rejoice.

I joy that from Thy love divine
   No power can part me now;
That I may dare to call Thee mine,
   My Friend, my Lord, avow;
That I, O Prince of life, shall be
Made wholly one in heaven with Thee.
   My portion, Lord, art Thou.

And therefore do my thanks o'erflow
   That one more year is gone,

And of this time, so poor, so slow,
   Another step is won;
And with a heart that may not wait,
Toward yonder distant golden gate
   I journey gladly on.

And when the wearied hands grow weak,
   And wearied knees give way
To sinking faith, oh quickly speak,
   And make Thine arm my stay!
That so my heart drink in new strength,
And I speed on, nor feel the length
   Nor steepness of the way.

Then on, my soul, with fearless faith;
   Let nought thy tenor move.
Nor aught that earthly pleasure saith
   E'er tempt thy steps to rove.
If slow thy course seem o'er the waste,
Mount upwards with the eagle's haste
   On wings of tireless love.

O Jesus, all my soul hath flown
   Already up to Thee;
For Thou, in whom is love alone.
   Hast wholly conquer'd me.
Farewell, ye phantoms, day and year!
Eternity is round me here,
   Since, Lord, I live in Thee.

A. H. Franke. 1691. [25]

[1] This chapter is published in a separate form, price twopence.

[2] Jacob Boehme (died 1624): "Wem Zeit ist Wie Ewigkeit, und Ewigkeit wie Zeit, Der ist befreit Von allem Streit."

[3] "We must go many times every day into the unseen world, and realize that we are there, much more truly than in our room, and in this present evil world." — Ötinger. Another Christian, says: "The first thing I desire to do in heaven is to thank God for having had so much heaven on earth."

[4] It is a commonplace remark, that time is short; but it is also true that time is long, and every day and hour a vessel into which immeasurably much may be poured before it is filled. The saying, "Time is money," is the true index of the worldly spirit. The Christian may say, "Time is eternity;" my moments are precious, because I live, work, and suffer for eternity.

[5] Heb. xii. 27; i. 14.

[6] T. Carlyle, *Sartor Resartus*.

[7] Goëthe's *Faust*, "Werd'ich zum augenblicke sagen," &c.

[8] I Tim. v. 6.

[9] All men, even the most successful, feel that there is something fragmentary and unsatisfying in every thing that is merely temporal. Goethe says, in his conversation with Eckermunn "I have always been regarded as exceptionally favoured by fortune, and I do not wish to complain or find fault with the course of my life. But, after all, it is nothing but labour and toil; and I may truly say that during my seventy-five years I have not had four weeks of real comfort. It is the never-ceasing rolling of a stone, which must always be lifted anew." (Quoted by Fabri in his suggestive pamphlet, *Zeit und Ewigkeit*.) This author also holds the following view: "Believers in Jesus have eternal life; by faith they behold and realize things unseen and eternal. Above this eternal life in time is the eternal life to which we look forward, when all that is imperfect and sinful shall have vanished, and we shall be in the perfect enjoyment of present eternal life. Below the eternal life in time is the region of death, in which there is no present (in the true sense of the word) and no future, but only the past. The past is remembered, the present contains no substance for the soul to dwell and to live on, the future does not exist; that is, there is no hope-no prospect of change." Thus Dante writes that the inscription on the gate of hell is, "Let all who enter here abandon hope."
[10] I John i.
[11] John iii. 3, 14.
[12] Rev. iii. 20; Hosea xiii. 4-7.
[13] Song of Sol. v. 2.
[14] I John ii. 28.
[15] "Men undertake to be spiritual, and they become ascetic; or, endeavouring to hold a liberal view of the comforts and pleasures of society, they are soon buried in the world, and slaves to its fashions; or, holding a scrupulous watch to keep out every particular sin, they become legal, and fall out of liberty; or, charmed with the noble and heavenly liberty, they run to negligence and irresponsible living; so the earnest become violent, the fervent fanatical and censorious, the gentle waver, the firm turn bigots, the liberal grow lax, the benevolent ostentatious. Poor human infirmity can hold nothing steady. Where the pivot of righteousness is broken, the scales must needs slide off their balance." — Bushnell.
[16] I John iv. 17.
[17] Cheerfulness is quite compatible with this aspect of the Christian character. (Compare Matt. vi. 16-18, Phil. iv. 4, &c.)
[18] Job i. 5.
[19] Matt. x. 39.
[20] Matt. xvi. 25.
[21] Mark viii. 35.
[22] Luke xvii. 33.
[23] John xii. 25.
[24] 2 Cor. v. 9 (orig.); Jude 21.
[25] Composed on his journey to Gotha after his unjust expulsion from Erfurt, as we are told in the oration delivered at his grave, "in the full experience of the unspeakable consolations of the Holy Spirit."

www.ingramcontent.com/pod-product-compliance
Lightning Source LLC
Chambersburg PA
CBHW051836040426
42447CB00006B/553